# MY "MESS OF A MARRIAGE" TO MY MESSAGE

"Since then, I've learned that how happy you feel is not a confirmation of how right your choice is..."

Copyright © 2016 Janice Fletcher. All rights reserved.

Published by Fletcher Enterprises, June 2016

www.linkedin.com/in/janice-fletcher-20220a11b

ISBN-13: 978-0692726945
ISBN-10: 0692726942

## CHAPTERS

PREFACE
ACKNOWLEDGEMENTS

### PHASE 1 – MARITAL MADNESS!
INTRODUCTION
1. FINANCIAL FIASCO!
2. STAND AT THE BACK OF THE LINE!
3. A CELIBATE MARRIAGE!
4. MAYHEM! MAYDAY!
5. "THE HANDWRITING'S ON THE WALL!"

### PHASE 2 – SEPARATION SOLUTION!
6. THROUGH JUNE GLOOM TO JUNE BLOOM!
7. WHOA! WHAT A MESS HE IS! OUR SESSION!
8. THE RESET BUTTON IS PUSHED!

### PHASE 3 – BACK ON TRACK!
9. MY JOURNEY BEGINNING – NO LONGER DERAILED!
10. DIVORCE DECISION
11. FROM MY "EX" TO MY "NEXT"!
12. WHY SO MAD?
13. DEDICATED TO DEDICATION
14. "WORSE THAN AN INFIDEL!"
15. HE'S NOT THE PRIZE!
16. "GOD DUST"
17. AN EPIPHANY!

### PHASE 4 – PARADIGM SHIFT!
18. "COURT'S IN SESSION!"
19. FORGIVENESS
20. NO JUDGMENT!
21. IT'S NOT OVER YET!

### PHASE 5 – "IT'S ALL GOOD!"
22. "A WAKE-UP CALL!"
23. PEELING THAT STINKY ONION!
24. "I FINALLY GOT IT!"

# PREFACE

I have asked the Lord many times for the reason that I went through this farce of a marriage. It wasn't His divine will for me to have a ten-month marriage to a man who <u>defrauded me both sexually and financially</u>! But in God's grace, He can take a mess and make it a message! And I have a message, even though it was initially my own journal, written to me, to get me through the disheartening marriage. But a message isn't a message unless it's delivered! So, my journal of my "mess of a marriage" has been transformed into a message to those who are going through any "messy" relationship, or to those who can be saved from going through any type of relationship "mess"! Hence, my memoir, <u>My "Mess of a Marriage" to My Message</u>.

"Reflections, Revelations and Resolutions"

My journaling led to a pattern of reflections, which led me to revelations, which then led me to resolutions. My memoir contains my journal entries that uncover and reflect on the things that a woman who is sexually and financially defrauded goes through, giving insight into the day-to-day drama that unfolds in such an unfathomable predicament. But more importantly, it uncovers my revelations and then my resolutions for my life as a wife. But a lot of these revelations and resolutions dealt with my state of mind prior to the marriage, which is what made me susceptible to the fraudulent marriage.

So while the reflections on the actual details of the marriage may be the most interesting to you, the reader, it is in the revelations – about what was actually going on, and then my ensuing resolutions – in which the message lies. I share my reflections in journal entry style by date in "this handwriting font," and the revelations and resolutions are found in "this regular font." These "revelations and resolutions" interjections may seem to interrupt my journal storyline sometimes, but I do resume each storyline in this font. Since this is a chronological memoir, not a topical book, my reflection-entries are prompted by drama and confusion that day. So, each entry unfolds with "Oh no he didn't!" reflections (ponderings), usually followed by revelation (inspired answers) that same day (changed to this font). Thus, subject matter jumps around a bit because it is an unfolding story, but I always get back to and tie together my reflections and revelations throughout my memoir.

I have barely edited my journal entries so that my book retains the authenticity of its memoir style. However, where you see brackets, "[ ]", I've inserted narrative during the editing process to expound or bring things current. Chapter titles and subtitles were also inserted for enlightenment.

Also, I might refer to something that is not explained in that entry, since I had not intended it for viewers, but as you read other entries, you will become more enlightened. This is because during my journal entries, I often flashed back to previous incidents that tie into the current entry, and I have labeled some of those. In fact, so many emotions and confusing behavior that I'd witnessed prior to my journaling were still unresolved in my head, so I do reflect back through many flashbacks. Through my flashbacks, I make sense of past confusing behavior based on what I'd learned since then, hence, I was able to make some revelations and some progress towards resolutions.

### "Revision Decision"

This is why I strongly suggest that you, the reader, embark on journaling if you find yourself in any unfavorable and confusing "mess" of a relationship. Journaling brings clarity and helps you to process the confusion and draw conclusions, leading you to your "revision decision", as I call it. This decision can be to establish boundaries, change the rules of the game, or end the game. You will see that the timeline from when I commenced journaling until I made and acted on my resolution was less than two months. Perhaps had I started journaling months earlier, I would have made the assessment that what had happened in my marriage was not alright, and I would have made my "revision decision" earlier.

My memoir is being published to help you learn how to reach your "revision decision" much sooner, before your circumstances lead you to a stress induced outcome. As you will learn after you get to almost the end of my memoir, although I thought that I had coped with my stressful circumstance via my "revision decision", my body thought otherwise. I experienced a stress induced physical manifestation, after having stayed under it for too long. I want you to reach your "revision decision" far before a stressful relationship takes an emotional and physical toll on you!

The names have been changed to protect the identity of all those involved, with the exception of my supportive friends, family and the three counseling professionals to whom I give thanks in the "Acknowledgements".

## ACKNOWLEDGEMENTS

To my pastor, Dr. Kenneth L. Gibson, of Point of Grace Christian Fellowship in Rancho Cucamonga, CA: I give so much credit to you for being my tangible-teacher and good shepherd! Your teachings are so insightful that they seem tangible! I'm always amazed at how skillfully you can break down a message to where I feel like I am actually there, amongst the biblical characters, witnessing their interactions. This helps me to internalize and remember teachings, even from years ago. And you provide such good care to your flock and to the community. Your good counsel upon my separation gave me great perspective. I only wish that I had sat down to counsel with you before I got married. I had a great resource in my life that I didn't use. My mistake!

To Dr. Jeraleen (Jheri) Peterson: You are a woman who so graciously combines compassion and wisdom. You give such sound counsel with a basis in compassion and teachings in boundary setting. You told me that I had become too accommodating. In hearing my story, you told me that even before my marriage, I had been too accommodating and available. You are right. And hence I surmised that being accommodating and marrying a user is the worst combination. Yet men who are users do seek out accommodating and available women...

To Dr. Travis Fultz, of Foothills Psychological Services: I'd like to thank you for the perspective that you shared in May 2014, when you told me that "It is not alright... what happened in the marriage." This led me to the conclusion that just because I'm a positive person who's trying to be strong, this doesn't mean that I shouldn't call it what it is and then make a plan to do something about it! It awakened me to the fact that my positivity had become my deceiver! This is profound! Then my own deception became the driver, not the Holy Spirit, Who was clearly telling me that what had happened was not alright! Yet for too long, I had listened to my positivity and what I thought was the "Christian" thing to do, instead of listening to the Holy Spirit, Who was sent by Christ to comfort and give wisdom!

You also told me that I "assume" too much. From that, I deduced that since I look for the good in people, I assume that they'll "do right" and correct their wrongs. So, I don't get an "A" for being "accommodating, available and assumptive"! I get an "F"; failure of my ability to discern that I was being played! This is why my revelations in my memoir not only point the finger at the man I married who defrauded me, but I point to myself for being a person who could be used to that extent! So my "revision decision" must also encompass a resolve to amend those ways, even though they may seem to be positive traits. Positive traits can still lead to vulnerability, when exploited by a user. So through the wisdom of the Holy Spirit downloading to me through journaling, I made the discoveries about what had gotten me off track to where I had become so vulnerable.

To my friends and authors, Teresa Batson and Karen Foote, who helped edit my book: I am blessed to call you friends. Teresa, your book "The Math Playbook" should be read by every parent who wants their kids to love math. Karen, your book, "Word Therapy" should be applied to every life... period!

Many thanks to my twin sister, Joyce, my "expert editor"; to my wonderful son, Jeremy, who showed me moral support after the separation, and to my wonderful daughter, Jeanine, who was my help in time of need. I must also give her credit in her gifting as a celebrity stylist and photographer, who did an absolutely wonderful job on my hair, makeup, wardrobe and the photography for my wedding (see cover photos)!

ACKNOWLEDGEES' CONTACT INFORMATION

Janice Fletcher and Joyce Fletcher:
FletcherEnterprises.consulting@gmail.com

www.linkedin.com/in/janice-fletcher-20220a11b

Dr. Kenneth L. Gibson: www.pointofgracecf.org

Dr. Jeraleen Peterson: www.wisdomtreecounseling.com

Dr. Travis Fultz: www.foothillspsych.com/TravisFultz.en.html

Teresa Batson: www.mathminded.biz

Minister Karen Foote: www.ministerkarenfoote.com

Jeanine Charis: www.instagram.com/dressupsesh/

# PHASE 1 – MARITAL MADNESS!

INTRODUCTION

*June 23rd, 2014*

*I feel like the cruelest joke in the world was played on me! And the "punch-line" of the joke hit on my wedding night! Now, it is inconceivable that I have been in a celibate marriage for nine months! It is a sad and sorry state of affairs that I found myself in! Yet, out of love and devotion, I stayed. But I stayed "assuming" that he would do his part in addressing the matter!*

*I felt like this since September 19th, 2013! This was when, on my wedding night, I discovered that my husband is <u>impotent</u>! After a long period of foreplay, I noticed that my new husband's penis never arose. In fact, I remember thinking that it seemed as though he were just going through the motions of giving extensive foreplay; it seemed devoid of passion. It just seemed like he was "doing his job", systematically going from mouth to breasts on down, but not really that into me. Then, he rolled over and held me and went to sleep! I was dumbfounded, confused, disappointed, hurt, etc.! It turns out, to him, "foreplay" doesn't mean "before" intercourse; it means "instead" of intercourse! I don't think I slept a wink that night! I decided to give him the benefit of the doubt and attribute it to being fatigued.*

*The next morning we tried again to no avail. And again, that night! At some point, I decided to ask him if he had something he needed to share with me. He said "No." I* brought up the fact that there have been no erections. He blamed it on several things. Me mostly! He said that he needs more stimulation. He also said that for a whole year, I've insisted on a celibate courtship, so how can I expect it to just rise now! [Actually, we had both agreed on dating without sex, based on our biblical beliefs.] I cried, because I just couldn't believe that "doing it God's way" could result in this. But I really didn't believe his excuse, so I pressed on, asking when he first noticed the ED. He tried to claim he didn't have ED, but admitted there were prior times that he didn't have erections. But he also claimed that during our engagement, he'd wake up at home with erections! I didn't want him to feel badly, so I didn't press the issue.

But night after night, after he'd gone to sleep, I'd sit in a bath of hot water in that big tub next to the bed [at a beautiful beach resort] and ponder the circumstance I'd walked into – and it kept pointing to the fact that Dick had <u>defrauded</u> me! He knew that he had a problem with erections, yet he did not tell me! In fact, he used to talk about how we were going to have to make up for lost time; how he'd come home stripping off his clothes and "do me" right on the kitchen counter, and how we'd have to get window coverings for the family room, because we'd be "doing it" in there all the time! He made me think we'd be very sexually active! He knew better, but he failed to disclose this critical piece of information!

But this isn't the only area in which I was defrauded. I was defrauded out of money. At the time, I believed that there was absence of malice; that Dick did not intentionally defraud me out of money. But the end result is the same. Thousands of my pre-marriage dollars were spent on marriage related items, when in fact, he was to have repaid me once married, but didn't. These pre-marital financial losses have compounded the "other" defrauding, and I just feel "ass-out!" I feel exposed, and the one exposing me is my own husband!

[So, this was the beginning of the end of our marriage – our wedding night! My story that I tell started on September 19, 2013, but my ponderings and confusion about what was really going on with him led me to take out my laptop and start journaling on May 1$^{st}$, 2014, which is where I begin. The introduction above is just extractions from a journal entry. Join me as I reflect back from the beginning to the end.]

## Chapter 1: FINANCIAL FIASCO!

*May 1$^{st}$, 2014*

It is the day after our 3$^{rd}$ major argument. Dick hasn't spoken to me. When he came in from work, he walked right into the kitchen where I was, as though he weren't going to speak. I spoke, and he responded with a dry "Hi." He's been in the living room watching TV and I in the family room watching "Burlesque", and now, "Black Coffee".

It started yesterday, when we were supposed to have talked "financials". Every time I say I'd like to talk money, he stalls it, because he knows he owes me money, both pre-marital and marital. [This is because the household expenses are on autopay through my credit cards, and our arrangement is for Dick to repay me half of these expenses on the first of each month.] Tuesday, I texted him saying I'd like to talk, but this time, Dick had a good excuse. We'd had strong winds that had blown leaves into the pool. I told him that I had skimmed the leaves thrice, and I asked him to vacuum the leaves that made it to the bottom - a 20 minute job. Dick proceeded to redo what I had already done, and then he vacuumed the pool and afterwards cleaned the filter. The tricky part is that I appreciated the extra attention he gave the pool, but I knew that after doing all this, he'd say he didn't feel up to having our talk. He'd want to clean up then relax. And that's exactly what he did; he did extra pool maintenance today to get out of the budget talk that I had requested.

But I stated that this was a planned talk. He kept asking what it was about. I said, "Our budget." After his shower, he came in and gave me only 15 minutes, so I showed him my credit card statements and spreadsheets and took a rain-check for the next day to finish. That next day after dinner, when I sat down and asked him to join me to talk financials, he just stood there with arms folded. I asked him to get his laptop and he said no. I asked him to sit down and talk and he wouldn't. He started right in on "I've gotta see this and that; I won't show you anything!" I reminded him that the night before, I'd shown him all our household expenses online via statements and spreadsheets.

He disregarded the spreadsheets and online statements, saying it's not what he wants. He stated that he wanted to see paper bills. He knows that all but two of the bills are paperless and paid through autopay, but he acts like he doesn't trust looking at our household bills on my laptop! To make it more concise for him, on spreadsheets I separate out our household expenses that we are to share, from those of my own; but he doesn't care for spreadsheets.

Then he asked for the only two paper bills we get: the light bill and cable bill (as though those two bills were all he was going to pay!). I told him to get them from the dining room, but he said he wasn't going in there to get them [a few steps away].

He kept saying "I won't stand for this!" Unbelievable! What won't he stand for? He makes that statement out of the blue! It always sounds like he's continuing an argument that he's had with another. Perhaps he's had budgeting problems in the past with one of his exes, and he is distrusting. Perhaps since he doesn't have a credit card of his own and is used to paying his bills with checks in the mail, he is uncomfortable with autopay. But it doesn't make sense for me to remove that feature and go back to mailing in checks, when he can just write me a check for half of what my credit card covered in household expenses.

But I conclude that he was being so unreasonable because it was all a cover-up. So I called him on it! Yet he just kept on asking for paper bills that he knew I didn't have. I asked him what he was hiding. He just kept repeating himself. He again asked for actual bills. I told him that's exactly what I showed him yesterday on my laptop; statements are itemized bills! Yet he objected to my spreadsheets and statements. So I went to open up my laptop to show him the credit card statements online again, but he objected to that and said he *didn't want to see it! All the time he stood there, unyielding, with arms folded! This is very defensive and elusive behavior.*

*His irrational behavior, inconsistencies in his demands and his refusal to show me his bank account reveal that he is hiding something. It was quite an eye-opener. So much so, that my eyes were open for most of the night. I was thinking for hours about what is going wrong here. He stayed in the living room, and I'd left the closet light on for him. But he stayed for hours, so I finally turned it off to see if the dark would aid in my drifting off. It didn't. So, the last night of April, I lay in bed, trying to sleep, but for hours I thought through our problems.*

I thought about sooooo much. The fact that he's hiding finances is not only a financial issue, but it is a character flaw. We're not having financial problems. We make enough money. We're having problems with his taking financial responsibility for half of our household expenses. That's what gets me. This is a huge issue for me... that he is willing to be dishonest with me and will try to displace the blame on me; additionally, that he isn't willing to take care of this household's financial obligations, much less, is he willing to take care of me. As I've assessed for many months, I'm not, and we're not his priority. However, as he should be, he is very willing to take care of his other households [kids from two ex-wives].

### FINANCES 101 FLASHBACK

*For the first few months of marriage, he contributed soooooo little. I was really caught off-guard by this. When single, he had been paying ~$1,200 in rent, (so I thought, but later he told me his dad was paying that) but once moving to my* house, he said he couldn't contribute this to our household. The first month, he gave me $200! I was so not expecting so small a contribution that I thought he was handing me spending money! LOL! I didn't know he thought this check was supposed to cover bills! It needed to have had a "1" in front of it! I told him that our expenses were far more than that, and he knew this from a pre-marital conversation about finances. I had created an expense spreadsheet and shown him. Somehow he was surprised at what it costs to run a household. He said he couldn't afford it, yet the surprising thing is that his half of the mortgage, utils and groceries would have been exactly what his former rent payment was: $1,200!

A few months prior to our marriage, he had gotten a temporary job, which was to become permanent with a raise in a few months. By the time of our marriage, this had not yet taken place, so he claimed he had little money to contribute. But I knew that even at the lower pay, he could afford the $1,200 and have several hundred dollars left; even after paying child support. Yet, September through December, he contributed only $200-$400/mo. I wanted to know why he contributed so little each month. I asked him month after month to show me his bank account, but he refused. This is early in our marriage and he's acting like this! It took him months (end of Nov.) for him to finally show me his account. I added up expenses and found that he was spending hundreds per month on lunch! He was eating out a lot, including a couple times a week at the cafeteria at ~$11 a lunch! This is a lot for a person who can't pay bills!

Mid-Nov, he got his raise, hallelujah! It would be reflected on his 1/1/14 check. But for the first four months of our marriage, Dick had not contributed to half of the household expenses (HHX). Therefore, starting in January, when he was in the position to play HHX catchup, I had him to contribute the $1,200 HHX/2 plus $700-$800 more through March to make up for the prior months.

I remember on March 1st, waking up that Saturday morning and saying to Dick that this is the month that he will finally catch up on his back HHX repayment! However, there was still $3k credit card (CC) debt from the previous months [African safari airline tickets, plus], and during that month, we had put an extra $1,460 on the CC for travel, pool supplies, dining and entertainment! So, he'd really have to continue to contribute more. [We had previously decided that since he makes almost three times what I make, when we generate bills above our regular HHX, he will cover it. Since he didn't have a CC, we used mine, and he was to repay me.] I had generated spreadsheets to show all this, and when I asked to show him April financials, he wouldn't let me. However, he had left a check for $1,867 one morning in early April. This was good for the HHX/2 of $1,200 plus almost half our extra expenses that month. So I paid on half of the extras and had planned to ask to show him the spreadsheets again.

In late April, my attempt to talk financials for May's bills and the continuing extra CC expenses met with the resistance I spoke of earlier. In fact, he later stated that $1,900 is too much for HHX. "That's a mortgage!" he said. I'm not sure that he remembers that the amount since January has been catchup on HHX. And in April and May we would have to cover our extra costs of $1,460 plus his new tire cost of $650. By the end of April, his $2^{nd}$ tire had blown out, so he got four new tires instead of just repairing them. He called me to come bring my credit card to pay for them. By now, he's gotten used to using me, and I have gotten used to being used! This should have been a wake-up moment!

[Resuming the May $1^{st}$ entry]

Following our blow-out argument yesterday, we did not talk all of today. He just sat in the living room watching TV, then fell asleep.


Friday, May $2^{nd}$, 2014

For the first time ever, Dick came home from work and came up to me in the kitchen and looked repentant and like he wanted to hug me! So I hugged him, and we didn't let go for maybe 20 minutes! This was the $1^{st}$ time he's ever said he's sorry! We ate dinner, and I stated he must have forgotten that $1,200 is his monthly share of the HHX and that $1,800 included extra for catching up and extra CC expenses.

## NOT LOW CASH FLOW, BUT LOW CHARACTER!

*Saturday, May 3rd, 2014*

*So, he left a check for only $1,300 today (not $1,800)!*

Again, we're having an integrity issue here. Even after his apology yesterday and my reminder of the CC "catching up" he needed to do, he still only put $100 towards it. He is keeping his income to himself. This is why he refuses to sit and talk money or show me his account. This reveals an even bigger problem, which is lack of character, lack of concern for our household, lack of concern and respect for his wife, etc.

But now I'm putting the pieces together. I'm reminded of a comment he'd made in February. He said that his income was his, not ours! And now I see how other confounding things that I'd seen months ago all come together... like that huge argument that we had when his kids were here for the week.

### Chapter 2: STAND AT THE BACK OF THE LINE!

#### FEBRUARY FLASHBACK

*Sunday, February 9th, we had an almost marriage ending argument.* His 2nd ex was having outpatient surgery earlier that week, and she had made arrangements to leave the kids with Dick. Dick had said just three days, starting Tuesday. BTW [by the way], this happened to be the same week we were scheduled to host three exchange students, so the house was full. The day before she had surgery, she had requested two more days. I wondered how, before she knew the outcome, she was already requesting more days!! Then Saturday night, I saw kids climbing into beds, instead of grabbing backpacks and heading for the door. Then this happened again Sunday night; so I asked Dick about it. He *said, "What happened last week – we'll just do it again this week!" I was shocked by the coarse way he decided to speak to me! I was disappointed that he consented to this without talking to me, and I was hurt by how he stated it with no consideration for how I might feel about it. I shared how I felt, and he was defensive from the beginning. I pointed out that he was defensive and that we should be able to talk about things without defensiveness.*

The times we have had to talk about anything, I've noticed his immediate defensiveness, as though he were picking up from where he left off with another person that he has history with. We really don't have history, and we surely hadn't argued before the first time that I'd noticed this. I believe he is taking the stance he did in arguments with his ex. He is projecting on me, based on how he interacted with his ex. Perhaps he learned to be defensive with her, and now that's his M.O. Perhaps she did a lot of attacking. Me, on the other hand, I don't attack. I ask for time to talk, then when we do, I just bring up the issues for resolution. The few times we've done this, however, he has been immediately defensive, and it turns into an argument instead of a discussion.

The other explanation for this is that he is guilty of something in each of these instances; hence his defense. He started right in on this phrase, which I think is his go-to defensive phrase, because I heard it for the second time, too soon in both arguments.

*He said, "I'm not going to stand for this!" I was wondering, "Stand for what?" I hadn't done anything to him; I was seeking understanding about how it is that three days turned into two weeks without my knowing. That is valid. But he escalated the tension by saying he won't have me treating his kids like this. Again, I hadn't treated them any way. They were in bed; he and I were talking in private. It was at that time that I saw a different face than I'd ever seen on him. I* told him that he had a look on his face as though he hated me.

He kept on with this behavior. I explained my position: that we'd agreed on three days only, then he told me about two more without agreement, then he didn't tell me about the next week until we were in it. He contended, "These are my kids! I'm supposed to take care of them!" I contended that if it is his ex's time to have the kids, and if for some reason she cannot fulfill her obligation, this doesn't mean it defaults to him! He believes it does. I said it is her duty to find someone to help her, not just have a "dad-default". She can't just expect him to pick up the slack without agreement from her ex and his next! He said it wasn't that she asked; he wanted to! I said, "Well that's a decision for us both." If that's how he operated when he was single, that's his decision; but now it's our decision, and he didn't consider me.

When I'm not considered, nor even told until the kids are here for two weeks, then I can never count on "us-time" to happen! This is really the basis of the issue. I had come to realize that he takes off his "husband hat" when his kids are here every other weekend. Therefore – with every cell in my body – I eagerly look forward to every week in between! I got married to have a relationship with Dick. I strongly desire that. And if he doesn't know how to share himself with me in front of his kids, then I'm left with resenting when they're here unexpectantly, and looking expectantly to alone time with my husband! However, the kids' presence is not the problem. It is his disregard for me and the unmet expectation of "us-time". His profession to me that day – that he will bring his kids here at any time, for any lengths of time without notice – in fact put me on notice that I cannot look forward to any set "us-time" with my new husband! It was quite a blow for this new wife who was so in love with her husband and just wanted to build our new life together.

This could really leave any of our plans vulnerable to his ex! This means that I have to base my schedule on her schedule! Ludicrous! I refuse to have my time, plans and household based her whims or even valid needs!

*He had done this before, exactly one month after our wedding, 10/19/13. It was my birthday, and we hadn't made specific plans for the day; since it was a Saturday, we expected to be spontaneous and take advantage of the whole day. Then he tells me we can't go anywhere until the evening, because his ex asked him to take Jill somewhere! I was shocked, hurt, betrayed, mad, etc.! I refused to have her change my birthday plans! He said that we had no plans. I said that we did: plans to spend the whole day out doing what we wanted... when we wanted! He's the one always saying he doesn't want to always have plans, but to be spontaneous; I complied... even on my birthday! I objected to the delay in our plans, and so he called her and told her he couldn't. I was so glad that he saw fit to let his ex down in lieu of letting me down! He probably sees it as letting his daughter down; but again, if she didn't get to go wherever it was, it was her mom who let her down, not her dad! It was her responsibility to get her daughter there. As it turns out, Jill just wanted to go to a friend's house, yet Dick was willing to cancel our birthday plans just to transport her!*

This set a precedent. It shook me really badly. It let me know that he was willing to put his ex's request in front of his wife's expectations, even on his wife's birthday! And even if he sees it as Jill's request, it is still imbalanced, because it was just her wanting a ride somewhere. But it was my birthday! A month into our marriage, he really showed me where I fit in! It was a rude awakening! And I saw many more instances of this since then.

I literally feel anxious when the phone rings and I hear him on the phone agreeing to stuff. I never know what it is, because he doesn't tell me until time for it to take place, and I never know if it is going to negate any plans that we have. And even if we don't have set plans, whatever we end up doing, it is supposed to be us... just the two of us. We only get two times a month to be together and go places. The other two weekends are his kids', and weeknights he's so tired that our only interaction is at dinner time. The rest of the evening he's in front of the TV. No problem with this, because he works hard and deserves some "downtime/me-time". I understand and support this, and hence, I wait for two weekends a month for "us-time".

[Resuming the February Flashback]

*So, he stuck to his stance that it is his obligation to take the kids whenever she can't. I contended that this is a problem. He said he'd just take the kids and go! I was shocked, but not surprised, because it only confirmed that I'm not as much of a priority to him. I just sat there and he did too, with a look of hatred on his face. I said, "So, it's true? What I've suspected is true! That I'm behind the kids in priority." He claimed that we're all equals; but I know better.*

Actually, I'm not in $5^{th}$ place; I'm in $6^{th}$ place! I come behind four kids and an ex! This is because, even if she's not in his heart, she still pulls the strings that involve [three of] the kids – and hence, our time!

<u>Anyway, it was the most eye opening interaction between us. I now am apprised of where I stand; it clears up the confusion I'd been feeling about his feelings toward me. I know my place; if I have expectations any different, then that is my fault! The only thing now is, can I accept this position, and how long does it last? Does it last until the last kid is out the house... in five years? Can I wait that long? Or is it until the last graduates from college? This means that for the next nine or ten years, I'll still be waiting to be his number one. Or is it never?</u>

[Resuming the May 3rd – "Stand at the Back of the Line" entry]

So, his lack of regard for the finances of this household stems from my being in 6th place, not first. I am not #1 in his heart, nor is our household, so we are not #1 in his pocketbook!

I can't change my #6 position. Only he can do this. But can I accept this position? Since February, I pressed on to do so; but now, not even three months later, I don't think I can. If it didn't keep manifesting itself, maybe I could keep talking myself into accepting it; but at least monthly, I'm going to be reminded of it due to his lack of willing contribution to our HHX. Add a few more interjections by his ex, a few more arguments that remind me of my 6th place, and a few weekends where he takes off his "husband hat", <u>I'll be running off fumes and prayers.</u> <u>This is no way to have a marriage.</u>

Currently, we're not depositing much here; we're just making withdrawals. Hopefully we'll pull it together soon, or the marriage will be bankrupt! So basically, if we are able to connect on our weekends and make a way to connect during the week, especially preceding the kids coming, we can maintain, or even grow. I've told Dick that I feel that we're stagnant, because we go backwards every other weekend because he doesn't wear his "husband hat" when his "daddy hat" goes on. But if we reconnect right afterwards, we go forward. But then we slip back the next "dad only" weekend. So we're stagnant. I've shared that when the kids are here, we need stolen moments and eye connection to keep from slipping backwards, so that we can keep moving forward in creating a stronger bond. If this doesn't happen, not only do we slip behind, but it makes me think I can't make it being his #6 for five more years! I need to have hope! That is a human prerequisite! I need something to make me think it's worth staying for.

*We need to work hard on making and keeping a connection during the weekdays, since we can't count on weekends. This weekend (Saturday, 5/3) he works all day; then Sunday he drives to get Jane [his oldest daughter] from college. Then next weekend we have all three kids [of his second ex]. But weekdays aren't any more reliable. I've noticed how when he gets home, his greeting is nowhere near the way it used to be. He says it's because he's tired after work. Yet before we got married, he'd come from work straight to my home for dinner, and back then he'd enthusiastically greet me, even though he was tired from work! For a while after we married, our greetings were still good. But for months now, he barely speaks, he barely looks my way, he has little to say, and he'd rather just go to watch TV.*

I respect his need to be alone, so all I expect is a greeting that says he's still in love with me. I haven't seen any indication of love in a long time. We talk at dinner, but that even seems strained — not organic like it used to be. So that's why I see that we're more like roommates now, sharing a bed. Well, if that's what it's reduced to, can I accept that? Will he ever fully place me as "wife" in his life?

Does he even see that I'm not fully "wife" in his life? He would never admit that I'm actually #6 or even #5. But if I get the leftovers of #5 (his ex's "daddy-default" strings), then I'm #6 in line. I get the leftover time after she dictates a schedule change. I get the leftover money, because she gets hers first. And naturally the kids get theirs first... time and money. I'm definitely #6. I stand in line. Again, can I live with this?

## HE PRESSED PAUSE ON US!

The conclusion I have come to is that he "pressed pause" on us. I think if he thought about it, he'd have to see this. I am at the stage in life where my kids are grown and on their own. I wanted my soulmate to grow with, do with, love on, be loved on, etc. His stage of life is child rearing. He had a tween when we got together. He is in the midst of launching his last, and that is where his energy is consumed. He is not even thinking past that. He has demonstrated that he can't wear two hats at once. Plus, they <u>are</u> his overall priority, and I agree that they should be (but can I get some love too?). Therefore, he worked hard at showing me attention and affection in our dating life, acquired me, then put us "on pause" until his kids grow up! As such, he doesn't have to put forth much effort anymore.

I can actually understand his point of view; but is it fair to me? Can I stay "on pause" for five to ten years?

What are my options? I'd rather it work out, so I must press on, even on "pause mode". What can make it better? His getting onboard with making our (1) connection a priority; (2) a determination to contribute to HHX and goals; (3) getting healthy under a doctor's care w/specialty in his problem areas; (4) travel; and (5) sex.

[I'd like to interject something here. On the back cover, I promised you that I would help you learn how to reach your own Revision Decision. At this point, you can see that I have already asked myself the same question many times. That is, "Now that I know what it is, can I deal with what it is?" So step number one it to assess what's going on through journaling your concerns and the puzzling behaviors you witness. After a while, you'll come to your, "It is what it is!" realization. Then you query yourself. Can you deal with what it is? If not, what are the changes necessary to enable you to deal with the relationship? If the other party isn't onboard with these changes, then what? Well above, I just expressed my wish-list, but that's not enough. So below, you'll see that I made a detailed list of changes that I'd need to see happen in order for me to stay in this relationship. Not that it mattered, because he was too defensive to even discuss such. Thus, another Revision Decision had to be made.]

(1) I can keep asking him to remember our connectivity ideals. Even if in a true 24/7, 365 connection isn't reflected in his heart, he can do things that make it appear that it is. Fake me out! At least it'll give me hope. He might even fake it till he makes it! Make me feel that you are still in love! That's every day, whether the kids are here or not. And I also need him to protect/guard our weekends for "us-time". Our weekends need to be reserved for us with either spontaneous or planned time to be out and about, or even to chill at home together.

(2) No more pulling teeth to talk finances. We shall have full disclosure of all income and expenses every month on the $1^{st}$ or $2^{nd}$, with full payment of our bills on time. We shall have full disclosure of all extra expenses that come up at the time that they come up, with a discussion and agreement on how or if we handle them.

Planning for savings is very important in our finances, and that must also be part of our monthly financial discussions; our agreed upon amounts should be saved monthly. In other words, contribute your $1,200 each 1$^{st}$, without complaint; let me remind you of any extra charges we put on my credit card and pay that; and let's save too!

Also, Dick must come clean about my capital outlay prior to marriage that he caused me to lose. I paid a $3k deposit on a safari trip we couldn't take because of him. I need that repaid. [Due to child support arrears, he couldn't get a passport.] There were several thousand dollars more that I paid out with the expectation that he repay me once his income increased. All that was pre-marriage dollars – my dollars! I want it all back!

(3) Dick's health is the most important. He must see a specialist for the health issues underlying his ED [erectile dysfunction] now and be under the specialist's regular care. He must also see the referred nutritionist and eat and take any prescribed meds as he should.

(4) Our international travel is on pause also until he resolves his arrears problem with child support services [CSS]. In the past I've asked him to make an appointment, but he didn't. Dick must meet with CSS and get his arrears issue straight so that he can qualify for a passport. We should plan for travel and save for travel, both domestically and internationally. I refuse to be held hostage by this passport/child support issue.

(5) Sex will have to be the glue. I tried to let affection and attention be its substitute, but he doesn't even give me that! And with all the other problems, I'm not moving forward without a change in this area. Between improved health under a doctor's care and taking Viagra, it should improve. He must be proactive about this.

### Chapter 3: A CELIBATE MARRIAGE!

*May 8$^{th}$, 2014*

*I've spent a lot of time recently thinking about the genesis of all our problems; but on the issue of no sex, I've spent a* whole lot of time. That's because it's not just the ED, but it is his lack of his desire for any physical contact... even affectionate expressions. We need a sex therapist. This area is moving too slowly, mainly due to him not taking how seriously this affects me. I've gone too long without sex... years and years at a time, just waiting for the Lord to bless me with a husband. Now I get one who has no sex drive! This is so devastating! If we at least had a sex life, I could see myself waiting on becoming #1. But no sex, no loving connection, no looking at me, no being turned on by me, no compliments that tell me he at least is attracted to me... I'm just perishing! Why did I get married? The two things I put off doing when I was single – which were to travel internationally and to have a sex life – I can't even do married! We are just roommates! Give me one thing to tip it over into more than that! Give me a sex life! But he can't.

### "GO FIGURE" – FLASHBACK

For the 1st few months of our marriage, I struggled through the impotence, waiting on the very day that we'd get medical insurance to get him in front of a specialist! So our non-sexual encounters consisted of rubbing and grinding to no avail. He'd always try to make it seem like I didn't arouse him, or he'd use a variety of excuses showing disinterest. I recall a time that I was grinding while sitting on top of him and he had a blank look, then he complained that I was hurting his penis. This could very well be... if the penis had been hard, it would have been inside me, not under me. Can't do much with a limp penis.

The other memory of his attempt to distance himself from sexual encounters was just a month after we were married, on my birthday. We attempted that Saturday morning, but as he often does, he complained that he was too tired (even though he had just awakened!). He said we'd try after we got back from our day out. He even added that we'd break out the whipped cream! That night, I brought the whipped cream in the bedroom wearing sexy lingerie and he looked at me like I was crazy. He asked what I thought we were going to do with that, and I reminded him that it was his idea. He scoffed at me and said he was too tired from being out all day! This was my birthday sex!

I've tried to get him the medical help he needs since Nov., when we got our medical coverage. I got a doc lined up and asked him to make an appointment for early December. He waited until the end of open enrollment to sign up, which pushed any possible doctor appointment until the end of December. I had spent hours researching the docs in the plan and found a primary care physician who had an endocrine specialty; which was probably Dick's need. But Dick resisted and went with another. This one happened to be 92 years old... and acted like it! I wanted to go to with him to make sure that the ED issues were addressed, but Dick wouldn't let me go to the appointment with him; I learned later that he didn't bring the issues up! The doctor told him to get lab work done and to return. Based on his lab work levels, the doctor told him to eat well and come back in weeks. All this had nothing to do with addressing the ED issue. Dick didn't even make an appointment to return for months.

We returned in March, and I saw how lousy this 92-year-old doctor was. I at least got him to refer a urologist, whom we saw on 4/1 and got Viagra samples. I'm reminded of my thoughts on my wedding night: I had decided to stay in the marriage pending Dick seeing a specialist, ASAP. This visit to a specialist occurred 6.5 months later! Dick has fought and refused to have his ED problem addressed, and I waited patiently for over half a year! [And this wasn't a specialist to address the root of his ED, just the symptom.]

The Viagra samples he tried did not work for him, yet we should give it a chance. He did follow up with the urologist this month and got more Viagra samples and a prescription. Here we are a whole month after seeing a specialist, and we're no closer. He hasn't filled the Viagra Rx, so we're still not progressing towards a solution. Later he told me that it isn't covered, but Cialis is, but he's heard of some side effects. Viagra isn't the solution though. He needs to see a specialist for his test levels, but he keeps putting it off. Dick agreed to change his primary care doctor, so I researched and found another endocrine specialist who is a prime. Dick refused to make the appointment though. He waited until the end of April to make a May appointment with him, and then he canceled it without telling me. He finally set a new one for June 11$^{th}$. We will have had coverage for over six months by then, and yet we're no closer to the solution.

He isn't taking seriously how this is affecting me! I am so sex starved, that I had dreams about infidelity twice. In March, I had such a vivid dream that I was being offered the chance to solve this problem by having an affair. I think in my dream it was the devil offering it. I struggled with the decision the whole dream, saying no, but my body was saying yes. Finally at the end of the dream, I chose yes. I woke up sooooooo ashamed! I was almost crying because I couldn't believe that in my subconscious I had decided to cheat, so as not to go without a sex life any longer. About a week later, I had another dream that I was tippin', and I thought no one knew. In the end, I learned that everyone knew, and they were quite disappointed in me. I'm also reminded of two dreams I had one night months ago. The more vivid of the two had us in a car, and I was driving this car without a steering wheel and dashboard - symbolizing that I had no control. A huge tractor or something started rolling over us; the hood was crushed, and we would have been next. I looked at Dick, and he was not even concerned; like he didn't understand the severity of the matter. I was panicking, trying to get out and trying to get him to agree to get out! We had a chance, but he wouldn't take it. I told him about both dreams, and he tried to trivialize it by saying that it showed that I worry and he doesn't. And then he asked why I was in the driver's seat. I answered "Because we sleep with me to the left; this dream signified us in bed, getting crushed by this ED problem. I'm suffering, but you're unaware of how big a problem it is!" Wow, it was so vivid and to the point! I told him it expresses how I feel about our sex life, and I asked him to please go see specialists. He promised he would do everything he could. Just on his own time... I see now!

This all tells me that it's past the point of dealing with on my own. We need a sex therapist! I am so serious. If he isn't willing, I'll go by myself! It isn't just the lack of intercourse; it is his lack of sex drive that equates to lack of interest in me. He isn't even turned on by me. When I put on something sexy, he doesn't even see me! There is no response in his eyes when he sees me naked! There is absolutely no response in his eyes! It is giving me such a complex. And what makes it worse is that when I go out, men tell me how great I look, but I come home and he doesn't even look at me. I even asked him to tell me if he ever thinks I look good. That was weeks ago; I guess I haven't looked good since! He could have even said it then, because I was looking hot! But he didn't. It really hurts; I'm in tears typing this. He used to say I looked good before we were married, but not anymore! I'm finding a sex therapist and starting sessions this month.

I've been at this for hours! It was just so necessary to get it out. Be back tomorrow.

## Chapter 4: MAYHEM! MAYDAY!

*May 10th, 2014*

Oops, I didn't get back to journaling the next day! I have neglected my entries, because my emotions have gone through extremes; when they were down, I did not want to revisit them through journaling. And then they seemed to work themselves out the times that Dick showed his better side. Yet those times were abbreviated with arguments over things I'd bring up that should have been just short and sweet discussions. My heart is very heavy over the fact that there is something much deeper going on that would cause my husband to react the way he does.

May 9$^{th}$ and 10$^{th}$, we had the kids, and they went home Saturday night to be with their mom on Mother's Day. I had a good outlook because I went into the weekend knowing that today, Saturday, I had a church event at Sister Ethel's home, so I didn't have to watch Dick and kids watch TV all day Saturday; Sunday Dick and I might have some "us-time". I returned from the luncheon to find them all in the family room watching movies. He didn't know it, but while at the luncheon I had told myself that as soon as I got home, I'd sit right here with Music Choice on the TV, while on my laptop to get some work done before our vacay. Not only could I not, but there were other issues. When I came in and spoke, Jack wouldn't look up and speak; he just kept his head buried into his texting. Jill looked right at me and did not speak, and Dick looked up and spoke under his breath. I felt this was all very disrespectful, and secondly, I had previously asked Dick to instruct his kids to speak to me. He has done so in the past, but he needs to correct it every time, not just once. The other problem was that my greeting was warm towards Dick, but he acted as though he wasn't willing to give a warm hello to his wife.

But the most apparent issue was that we had previously agreed on the kids watching TV in the living room, leaving the only other TV open for the adults in the house. I don't watch their kid shows, and most of the time I want to just listen to Music Choice [the cable box is only in the family room]. With them watching the living room TV, I'm not displaced every other weekend, and I can go about my routine of music or my own TV shows. In fact, Jill was going back and forth between both rooms for two TV shows, so even if I wanted to use the living room instead, I couldn't; Dick wasn't considerate enough to address this. The family room unites the areas that I occupy, so to have it off limits to me really interrupts my functioning in our home. I went to my room and stayed for as long as I could, but couldn't stand it any longer. I bailed. I just went out to a store, and when I was finished, I just sat in the parking lot for hours. This isn't the first time I've had to do this... to avoid being confined to my room which is the only room not overtaken by the loud and wacky sounds of kid shows. At least I had the beautiful mountains as scenery; not just the four walls of my room! Not that I don't want interaction with Dick's kids, but you can't interact with someone whose eyes are glued to kid shows... all... day... long! This whole scenario just points to Dick's unwillingness to consider me in the household.

When I returned, Dick wasn't speaking to me. I thought this was a good time for us to do "us", since we had the house back; but he was cold, and I don't know why, since I had not said anything about how the prior incident had had made me feel. I just left, telling him that I'd be back later.

Monday, May 12th, 2014

On Mother's Day, he still was not speaking. Yesterday morning, I saw that Dick had left a card on the bed. I saved it for the brunch that Jeanine [my daughter] had reserved. He wasn't talking though; I was never told "Happy Mother's Day." Jeremy [my son] came over and rode with us to church, and then we were to meet Jeanine at Marie Callender's for brunch. While waiting on her and waiting on our table, I asked Dick about his being distant and aloof, and he claimed he wasn't. I asked him if he could stand by me and even touch me. He mechanically held my hand but wouldn't look my way. His behavior and pretense were so hurtful. Since we had my kids to talk to over brunch, it wasn't that apparent that we weren't on one accord. But he continued his silent treatment towards me. He even sat there and let my daughter pay his bill! [What a big baby!]

That evening, it was time to take his mother and me out. On the way, I broke the silence by asking him if he'd tell me why he was mad at me. He ignored me. I asked him please not to let these feelings spill over into our vacay [the next day], but he still wouldn't participate in any resolution. I asked him to share just three things; one now and two on the way home. He ignored me. I told him I didn't want to have to pretend to be in harmony in front of his parents. He said he just wanted to enjoy his wife on the way. I said that there was no enjoyment in the tension. He said there was no tension; we weren't as close as other times, but there was no tension. He is in serious denial. He hadn't touched me, talked to me or even looked in my direction for days, and he thinks that doesn't cause tension.

He had not told me where we were going, and when I saw it was another buffet, I told him I couldn't eat a thing, being stuffed from the 1st buffet. I just sat there and talked with his family without eating.

## VACAY! YAY!

*May 19th, 2014 [Journal entry after vacay.]*

He kept up the silence until our Puerto Rico vacay, the next day. It wasn't until we were on the plane, that I saw him change back. He started talking to me like nothing had been wrong before. He smiled, touched and actually looked at me. I just went with it... no questions! So we were good the rest of Monday and Tuesday when we got there.

Tuesday night, I changed into an outfit he'd never seen before, and it was très sexy. Again, there was absolutely no spark in his eye when he saw me; I did not evoke any response at all! But then I put on large dangling earrings, and I got a response about how heavy they must be! I tried to put it behind me... the notion that he can't acknowledge my sexy outfit, but he can acknowledge the supposed weight of my earrings!

I know that I look good, but since he has no sex drive, I need to know that at least he is attracted to me. The ED is due to a medical condition, but he should at least still be turned on by me and still be interested in sex with me, even if he can't. It should register in his eyes at least, even if it doesn't register in his penis. And it should definitely come out of his mouth!

This is so important to me, because without a sex life, I need to know that there is still some life in our marriage – some hope! I need something to feed off of. If he is not interested in me sexually, then getting his ED addressed is futile, and the marriage is also futile. I need to know if there is anything there.

*That is why, twice in mid-April, I'd asked him to please compliment me if he ever sees me looking good to him. He never did since then. Sometimes, after the fact, even days or weeks later, he'll say I looked good, but never on that day, and never does it register in his eyes at the time. When we've talked about this before, he says stuff like, "Well, you're a good looking woman." Just a generic assessment; not, "Baby, you turn me on; you're so sexy tonight!" or anything like that. He says it's not what I'm wearing; I'm good looking always, so he doesn't have to say it. Well he does, because even though I know I look good, I need to know that I turn him on... there's a difference. I want him to think I look sexy, feel turned on by me, and say it!*

It's very telling that he doesn't understand the concept of a man being turned on by his woman. His response to the issue of him noticing me is that – I am generally attractive. Well, grandma is generally attractive every Sunday! But a woman wants to know that she turns her man on! She needs to see and hear this! Yet Dick doesn't get that, because I believe he isn't turned on by women – period! I'm beginning to think that, though he appreciates women (and their capacity to give him children), he is no longer turned on by them. So at least he's being honest by not complimenting me. There's no <u>rise</u> in his pants or in his <u>eyes</u>; so to express anything more would be <u>lies</u>!

*This kept bothering me that Tuesday night, so after we left the concierge desk, I asked if I could talk to him. We sat* downstairs near a staircase, and as soon as I brought it up, he said he knew that's what this was about! So, he knew that he should have complimented me instead of picking on the supposed weight of my earrings! This was done intentionally to provoke me! Then he said, "You looked in the mirror and saw you looked good, so why do you need me to tell you!" He said I need to concentrate on why it is that I have such a low self-esteem as to need to be affirmed by someone else!

I couldn't believe a simple cry for a life-line to our marriage turned into an argument! I thought he'd just acknowledge his sexy wife, and we'd be off in less than a minute. It wasn't supposed to take long, and it certainly wasn't supposed to turn into this! He asked "Do I have to say you look good even if you don't?" I told him that was hurtful, but he kept asking it; so I answered "Yes." He got worse with it, talking loud and wagging his head as he was saying these hurtful things. At that time, a couple was coming down the stairs, so I told him so he'd stop and not embarrass me. He wagged his head and said "I don't care if someone else hears me!" I was through! I got up and walked outside and had a talk with God. I was overwhelmed with emotion. That was our 1$^{st}$ night there and thus my 1$^{st}$ night walking out into the warm night... seeing the romantically lit landscaping and hearing the millions of birds singing to me. I was overwhelmed with beauty and sensuality surrounding me, yet with the lack of beauty and sensuality in my life! There was so much dissonance, and I felt I needed to break that dissonance! I needed the negative circumstances to correct themselves and line up with the beauty that is supposed to be in my life. I didn't get married to have such discord; I chose the man who purported himself to be the best man in the world for me; so things aren't supposed to be this way! And though things will never be perfect, a mate should be able to bring up those things that can and should change without discord arising! I said to God, I didn't want this man anymore! I don't know who he is. He certainly isn't the man he had led me to believe he was, and I don't want him!

Our repeated discord — arising out of his defensiveness when I bring up something — resulting in hurtful comments and behavior — is certainly worse than anything that he had done that I had brought up! In essence, he has me in check... not to say anything about anything! That's the only way to have peace! But I will not live like that! There are two people in this relationship, and each has to be able to participate, whether in speech, in sex, etc.

So, the rest of the week, I had a resolve! I am not holding on to this marriage any longer under these conditions! And I decided that he wouldn't ruin my fab vacay either! I had a new attitude! I went about as though he weren't there at all; not to be mean, but to preserve the integrity of the rest of the vacay. Enjoyment and tension can't coexist. I opt for enjoyment. He did the same... acting as though I wasn't there; which is the same as how he acts most of the time anyway. So for the rest of Tuesday night through Friday night, we were two souls riding in the car together, doing things together yet apart. He was busy taking "selfish-selfies", instead of including me or turning his camera around and taking pics of his wife. I wasn't like that. I took pics of him... many! I had to ask him to please take some of me with my camera to catch more of the beautiful background, *even though I was voluntarily capturing him in the beautiful sceneries.*

*Tuesday night, we took off for Old San Juan, even though he knew he'd left the directions back at the room. We got lost for hours and never made it there. By that time, all the restaurants were closed, except for a Chinese food restaurant in a casino in San Juan. We ate in silence. When we walked out, he asked if I knew how to get back. I said, "No; I use directions, I don't guess." He turned and went back inside to ask; leaving me out there alone. He took a very long time, and it bothered me that he was so willing to leave his wife outside a casino in a foreign city by herself.*

<u>There are just things that I pick up on that don't look like love to me. Even more so, they don't look like a "man" to me. A man protects his woman; yet all Dick does is expose me! At best, I'm thinking that he is very much like a child who just hasn't grown into a man. At worst, I'm beginning to think that he just has few masculine qualities. His lack of masculine predisposition perhaps betrays something deeper. He's more like a female to me than my man, whose instincts would tell him to be into me and to protect me. So I go on pondering this thought, which his inactions over the months (in and out of bed) have planted in my mind. He's just not "manly". He is not turned on by his attractive wife who loves him; his instincts don't tell him to protect his wife; he even argues like a girl – wagging his head and all!</u>

[I had underlined this journal entry because it was the beginning of another line of questioning in my mind. Just more things that were coming in my mind for assessment...]

*Wednesday morning, we were supposed to go to the time-share breakfast on the $7^{th}$ floor, but he said that he had an upset stomach. I went up there to reschedule it, and then I found a place for breakfast. I walked around looking summery-*

sexy in the long skirt I had borrowed from Jeanine, with no one to appreciate it. He was up when I got back, and I gave him the mints I had brought back for him. He showed no appreciation for my consideration, and instead of saying thanks, he said, "Mints don't help me!" These insensitive encounters keep fueling the discord!

I changed clothes, and we went out in search of something to do prior to our evening Bio Bay tour. We drove around, found things to see, found Fajardo Beach, and there we found the backside of the Waldorf Astoria. We went around to the front and got in on the splendid grounds. This is where his selfish-selfies began. BTW, "selfie" doesn't mean a picture taken by yourself; it means a picture taken by your "self"! There can be two of us in the picture! I say this, because it wouldn't occur to me to take pics of only myself when I'm on vacay with someone else. I don't think like this. Even though we're not relating, we'd still want some good pics of our vacay. I decided to speak up and ask him to take some of me, and he did. I did notice that his postings were mostly of himself on his vacay, but mine were labeled "Our Vacay", and it showed us both! When he saw how great my album was, then he tagged some of us and posted us. [I've since then removed him from my vacay album and relabeled it!]

We had lunch at a home-restaurant and had our first taste of Mofongo. Too expensive, and not even that good. Our Bio Bay tour was great! We cooperated with each other to row the kayak. Afterwards, we discovered Pincho Campera and enjoyed the fish kabobs and creamy Pina Colada!

*Thursday, we had our catamaran scheduled for 9 am, so we got there and enjoyed the waters. He was not speaking to me and laid out a lot (he had sea sickness). I was on my own then and thoroughly enjoyed myself! I didn't hesitate to hand the camera to him for shots. We snorkeled on our own, and then I had another experience that exposed his lack of manly predisposition to protect his wife. While snorkeling, I got too far out and panicked. I shouted for help to the nearest person from our group on shore. This man offered to throw his preserver, but it didn't make it to me. For the longest, I didn't know that this man was Dick, because with my glasses off, from afar he looked Caucasian. [It is interesting that, because we don't have a sex life, I was not familiar enough with his body to have even noticed before that his body (which doesn't get much sun) was so much lighter than his face.] Furthermore, I would have thought that if my husband had heard me hollering for help, he would have jumped in to save me! Boy was I wrong. He was so casual with his attempt to help me that I didn't think it was him!*

*Friday morning we went to the timeshare breakfast. It took hours, so by noon, we made an exit and tried to schedule zip lining by phone, but there was no answer. We decided to drive to Old San Juan. We still weren't relating, but made comments when we'd see something that caught our interest. We toured San Cristobal Fort for hours. Then we drove, parked and walked to El Moro Fort. When it closed that evening, we left and found a cute outdoor restaurant and ate with the cats. Yes, for some reason, the Old San Juan* outdoor restaurants are filled with cats! By now, though we still weren't relating, we were not silent. We'd made enough commentary about our surroundings that it substituted for conversation. And with the beauty around us, it felt like harmony! It was close enough! I don't want to settle for this being us, but it was certainly a better "us" than earlier in the week! After dinner, as we continued to walk around, I was very much feeling like I wanted to hold hands, but I just couldn't make that leap. He doesn't show interest in me like that; we're more like roommates, not even friends. I think holding hands at that point would have been artificial. Since we had passed the stage of pretense months ago, I didn't know if I should risk having him do something that he wasn't feeling. After all, if he wanted to hold hands, he would have; he knows me and my desire for affection. I thought, "Then why don't I ask him if he wants to?" I couldn't find a way to work that in. In fact, I decided not to, because every time I bring up something to improve our standing, it turns into rejection. Remember, the silent treatment from Tuesday night to Friday night was due to my asking him for acknowledgement! Instead of getting a compliment, I got the silent treatment through the next four nights!

We did a lot of walking around Old San Juan, shopping at the Haitian gift store and finding another gift store to buy shirts for the kids. When we got back to the resort, after my shower, Dick was sitting at the end of the bed with lotion, and he massaged my feet - real well! He also worked his way up, and we had "intercourse-less" sex! Needless to say, we were back! This was after midnight, Friday night, so it was only Saturday and Sunday that we actually had our vacay "together"! Saturday, we went to the El Yunque Nat'l Rainforest. We were as one, and the pics depict this. It was wonderful! We found a stream and bottled some water, and found La Coca Cascades, then found a trendy restaurant on the way down. Then we showered and dressed and headed back out for our fish kabobs.

Sunday, we headed for central Puerto Rico to zip line "The Beast"! It was so fab! "The Beast" is the fastest, highest, longest zip line in the world, and you ride it "Superman" style. It felt like I was flying over the rainforest! Then we toured the Camuy Caves. Then on the way back, I changed to a dress and heels in the car, and we hit Old San Juan in style! We found the old art museum with a restaurant inside. Then we walked and walked. We were on one accord, and it was beautiful.

Monday, we found a place on restaurant row in Luquillo Beach to have breakfast. Our last meal was the best meal while there! I had pionono, a fried, meat stuffed plantain sandwich – yum, yum! A pleasant surprise ending to our trip was the arrival of two baby parrots. The owner let us take pics with them… so cute! We returned our car and made it to the airport in plenty of time. We had upgrades on two flights; one of those was 1st class baby! Lunch and flowing wine! We arrived home safely! Thank God! Praise God!

<u>Wrapping this up, had I known that simply seeking acknowledgement of my sexiness to him would have caused him to reject me for the first four days of our vacay, I never would have asked! Again, it is all about seeking clues to dispel my mounting concerns that he's just not that into me. The</u>

<u>lack of acknowledgement when I am looking that sexy is rejection in itself; but what ensued after I asked for a compliment was far more than rejection. He insulted me, embarrassed me, and then totally rejected me. I just thought of this... this is abuse! He has totally manipulated me with his passive-aggressive behavior!</u>

Backtracking a bit to that night after he'd refused to compliment me and we were lost for hours and ate in silence; when we were in bed, he made a statement that I'd never heard from him... that I'd longed to hear from him. Straight from the lines of the movie, "Baby Boy", he said, "I was wrong, I won't do it again." That's all a woman really wants. We don't expect perfection; we just expect a profession of wrongdoing and a determination not to repeat the same wrong. He went on to say, "You did look nice tonight." I thanked him and we went to sleep.

I really did appreciate his saying that, yet he proceeded to repeat the same insensitive behavior the rest of our vacay! I was looking sexy the entire vacay! Every outfit I wore, even daytime, was sexy, off the shoulder, tight and short... and he'd never seen any of them before. [My stylist daughter had picked out several pieces from her "DressUpSesh" collection!] He would not compliment me or even look at me. I wore two different swim suits that week that he'd never seen before. He didn't bother to acknowledge me in them. A real man knows to acknowledge his woman in a swim suit! When we were at the pool and Jacuzzi, I noted how many men's women had love-handles and muffin-tops spilling out of their bikinis, but their men were all over them, initiating affection and looking at them when talking to them. I was intently *looking at these couples and how their men were so into them; but my man couldn't even look my way.*

## SEX 101!

It occurred to me that for men, attraction starts at the penis level and then rises to the eyes. Yes, men are visual, but they see with their penises. If they have a healthy physical relationship with their woman, her very presence turns them on, and it shows in their response. It has less to do with how she looks and more to do with their sex life. So all this time I've been asking for the secondary response via compliment to prove the primary sexual attraction. But if the primary sexual attraction is not present, it would be a lie for him to ever tell me that I turn him on. Any compliment would be a general acknowledgement of beauty; as one who acknowledges a beautiful flower. That's why he asked if I wanted him to tell me I look good to him even when I don't. He was honest! I don't look good to him the way that a man is attracted to a woman!

A man who is having sex with his wife appreciates her just for that! That keeps him close to her; being affectionate based on the sex they had last night, or the sex he hopes to get that night. Sex is the glue. He's going to do what it takes to keep it coming. And the ecstasy he feels those times is on his mind... those times when he's feeling her up in public and looking in her eyes and paying her attention. If a man is not having sex with his wife, then she is just his roommate, and all that attention/affection stuff doesn't even apply!

So it goes back to sex. Not whether he thinks I'm sexy or not, and certainly not whether he acknowledges it or not. In my mind, I had thought, "Well, in the absence of sex, if he still finds me desirable, then we have something to work towards." <u>But that's backwards; he needs to fix the sex problem first, then he will appreciate the one he has sex with... and will start to show it! The ED not only prevents us from having sex, but it prevents his desire to have sex, thus his desire for me!</u> So I'm asking him to do the impossible. Fake interest! That's why he asked, "Even if you don't look good, you want a compliment?" He is really in a non-masculine mode, dictated by his ED, and his body and mind don't pick up on sexual cues like other men. Men who are sexual pick up on the shoulders out, and tight white jeans, and toes out in heels, and dangly flirty earrings. (Remember Will in the movie with J Lo, "Hitch", saying he knows she's not out to pick up a man, based on her flats and tiny earrings? Masculine men know the cues.) When I come out the bathroom dressed in something provocative, it does not provoke him! It does not register on his sensory apparatus. And even though I know what that apparatus is, and I know that his doesn't work, I thought, "Well, his eyes still work, and so does his mouth; so he should speak it!" But no; a man's apparatus/penis is what tells his eyes and mouth to react. But in Dick's case, his dick doesn't work, so his eyes and mouth won't follow. I know, because each time, I intentionally look into his eyes for a response, and there NEVER is one! I do not turn him on!

Now in some other context and conversation, his typical and infrequent compliment type is that my dress is "spiffy" or "summery", or "nice". And two out of those three times it was because I asked how I looked. Of course I was fishing for "sexy", but got "spiffy" or "nice". Oh, and there was another instance when, a month later, he shared that I had looked sexy at a party we'd gone to. I asked him why he didn't tell me then. Again, he answers, "I thought you knew."

*This was the time that Dick had to pick up his son from the airport, so he dropped me off at the party, then left and returned. When he left, men lit on me, telling me how good I looked and some looking like they'd like to go farther. I was hot, in my hot pink mini dress and stilettos. And this was Dick's first time seeing me in it, but he never commented, nor did his eyes show any response. It bothered me that these other men could find me attractive to the point of walking over to me and telling me, but my own husband couldn't.*

See, he is clueless due to his apparatus not working. When the apparatus works, just the rising of it makes a man automatically make a sexy comment to his woman. The words are indicative of the physical response to the stimuli. So, my knowing has nothing to do with it. I know I look sexy, but I want to know that I'm a turn on to YOU, WHEN it's happening! It is not that I want to know in general that he thinks I'm attractive. I think flowers are attractive. The sky is attractive. Granny in her Sunday's best can look attractive. Women can look attractive, but I'm not attracted to them! I want to know that he is ATTRACTED TO ME! It should be revealed in his eyes, speech and behavior, but it doesn't, because it never registered on his apparatus. So his mind tells him a general acknowledgement, "yeah, she's attractive." But these after the fact, "spiffy, summery and nice" compliments still don't tell me that I move him.

TOO MUCH, TOO LITTLE, TOO LATE!

*May 24th -26th, 2014*

*Dick wasted four days in Puerto Rico with us apart, and we finally had two days as a couple. This is insane, and this demonstrates how he is willing to operate in dysfunction, even to the point of wasting a vacay!*

*We returned, on May 19th, our eight-month wedding anniversary. He continued the interest in me, even going back to pre-marriage levels! Hey! He'd come up behind me, feel me up, kiss me, look at me when he's talking, and a couple of times, when he was putting me in my car, he was all over me. This was so good, and I thought it could last. Maybe he felt badly about wasting our vacay and decided to be nice. I was hoping that it would continue into the weekend with the kids, instead of reverting to "daddy only". He did a remarkable job! He was really on it... wearing his "husband hat" all weekend!*

Another bonus was that, since Jack had something going on Friday night, the kids didn't come until Saturday morning. That gave us a bonus Friday night! I thought this would be a good time to retire early and try to get-it-on. That wasn't his thought. He thought, "Let me stay up watching TV and look at my vacay album on Facebook!" I even intimated that it would be nice if we used this kid-free Friday night to get busy, but he preferred TV and Facebook.

Saturday morning we did get busy; our intercourse-free version, of course! Jane and Jack came by noon, but Jill had spent the night with a friend. Dick was going to take them to an event at his job, but didn't. We hadn't grocery shopped since our return, and he didn't prepare for the kids, so I went and got food and we all had a good long time talking over lunch. Dick worked hard on the front yard and washed my car. He was showing sexual attention when he put me in the car to go to the gym. It was niiiiiiiiice! So, it is becoming apparent that he can turn it on and off. But when it's on, does that mean it's fake?

On Sunday morning, Dick had attempted sex to no avail again, so we got up late, and I went to church alone. The kids just watched TV all day. Monday we went to his parents' house for Memorial Day. We spent 9.5 hours there, and it was an enjoyable time. I saw his baby and kid pics. I gave his mom a tall bottle of luxurious lotion as a personal gift, and we gave his parents a souvenir from Puerto Rico. Dick had given the kids their souvenirs without me. I thought they were from us both. I had laboriously peeled all the stickers off the labels, getting them ready to present (I was actually the one who picked them out in Puerto Rico and paid for them), and he didn't give me the satisfaction of being present for the presentation. Even in his good state, his overall modality makes it such that he operates in the exclusive mode, not the inclusive mode. So the action is just a sign. I wouldn't complain that he didn't include me, but it is just indicative of his "family vs. wife" modality.

This weekend was easy, because we had come off our vacay, and because he was acting married that week and carried it on even with his kids here. Also because were out all Monday; we weren't stuck in the house all weekend! Thank God for a good weekend as a family! That's how it should be with a blended family. That's why they call it "blended"! Dick never facilitated blending.


Tuesday, May 27th, 2014

Things were still good between us. This morning, he got up early to get his kids out, then got in bed behind me and we spooned. From work, I got a text asking if I'd be naked when he gets home. I said, "Of course!" and was thinking, "I've got my man back!" I really thought I had, but – Not! When he returned, I was naked in the kitchen. I had decided not to start dinner since he'd suggested that he wanted to be intimate when he returned, but he got back late, so I had gone on and started it. I asked what he wanted to do, and he said he wasn't hungry. He didn't look interested in sex either; in fact, he didn't look at his naked wife besides the first look. He kept looking in the family room instead, so I said something, and he replied, "Well, you're in the kitchen!" I said, "Well take me where you want me to be!" He took me to the bedroom and we stood at the foot of the bed and the embrace was sooooo mechanical! He was barely touching me, but we kept on hugging and kissing. Then he laid me on the bed and attempted sex. He couldn't get the head in using the splint method with his fingers the first few times, but he kept trying. When he was able to splint the head in, he attempted a stroking action, and the head pulled out immediately. He was never able to get the head back in. He kept using his fingers as splints, which only irritated my vagina, but I never said a word. Then he rolled me on top of him and told me to put it in. He knows that his limp penis can't go in that way. The only way he's ever gotten even the head in is "froggy" style, while using his fingers as splints alongside the head. It made me wonder about his level of denial and also if he is he trying to make me take some of the blame. In his mind, is he saying, "Well, I asked her, but she wouldn't put it in!"

## TALK TUESDAYS TAILSPIN!

Afterwards, over dinner, I shared that I had wanted to initiate "Talk Tuesdays". I began with a huge compliment on his keeping up the husband mode the previous week and through the weekend with his kids here. He appreciated this. I told him how he reminded me of how he was before we married and that I'd longed for him to return to this mode.

I transitioned into stating that there were other things I really wanted him to return to. I told him that before we married, he'd been so good about taking care of business and in a timely manner. These were things I'd asked him to do as well as other things that he proactively did. I gave examples of things I'd been asking of him... one being of going to the doctor. He balked at this, saying he's gone to one (the 92-year-old with dementia). We talked about the fact that the urologist prescribed Viagra, but that he won't fill the prescription and won't take the six samples he's had for a month! He said he took one the other night when the kids were here (I had wondered why he initiated sex out of the blue). He said it worked at 3 am when I was asleep! I told him he'd need to include me next time. He had told me the same thing a month earlier, when he had the first sample pack. I said a solution would be to take it much earlier, so that it kicks in when we're up. He said it's not just that it needs to kick in, but that he needs stimulation. I reiterated that if he'd time it, I'd be awake to stimulate him. He's smarter than that. I think he was trying to insinuate that I'm ineffective at stimulating him. I didn't go there with him. (P.S., not true that he needs stimulation, since it supposedly rose when he was asleep!)

He said that I bring up the doc too much. But I said that I barely do monthly, and monthly isn't too much when your loved one has health issues. I told him I loved him and wanted him healthy, and that his health affects me - directly. I said I wished he could appreciate the fact that I have contended with the ED for over eight months, and he is not willing to be proactive with a doctor's care. He complained again and also started counting the things I was bringing up. He even said he's never gotten this treatment before; insinuating that his other wives were very happy with all his behavior. I ignored this too. But I should have retorted that at least his other wives were getting some!

I also reminded him of the money he owed me for paying his son's prom fees when he didn't have the money. He said he'd pay me back, but didn't. I told him that as much as wanting the money back, I wanted him to be proactive in getting it back to me and thanking me. He said he forgot.

I also brought up the fact that on Mother's Day, though he gave me a card, he never treated me for that day, or so much as even said "Happy Mother's Day." He snapped, "You're not my mom!" I said that's a hurtful thing to say; I told him that people who weren't my kids said it and texted it to me. I also reminded him that my kids took me out to brunch and paid for my meal and his. I said this wasn't right. He should have paid for his and even part of mine. He said, "We've discussed this before." Not entirely though, and he hadn't said he'd pay it back. This time he said he would. [The prom fees plus repayment for Jeanine paying his brunch bill came to over $100, but he eventually only repaid me $100. Of course I repaid Jeanine, so I was actually stuck with having paid part of his son's prom fee! Ludicrous!]

But he continued saying I'm not his mother, so he wasn't the one treating me! He said his treat was when he took his mom out; if I had eaten, he would have paid for that too. But I couldn't eat a second buffet in the same day, and he knew I couldn't. He repeated "You're not my mother!" The first time he said this I told him it was hurtful, but he said it two more times. Then he said I need to "check my feelings" if this hurts! It got so ugly. He asked "What do you want me to do?" I reminded him that he not only didn't give me a birthday gift or Christmas gift, he didn't give me a Valentine's Day gift, and now, nothing for Mother's Day. In the past I had asked that he make up for the other missed occasions. I wanted to say it this time, but he had gotten so ugly by then that I didn't. I just said that it wasn't acceptable that he not get me gifts for one occasion after another.

He has said in the past that he didn't have the money, but I know his take home pay, and I know our expenses. So he does have it, unless there is more money he's giving away to his other households that I don't know about. But, he will spend money on himself. I noted how he went out and bought a new cologne for himself months ago, but wouldn't pick one out for me even though I had been asking for a belated gift! He will include me on his food bill if he's paying, but he doesn't intentionally spend money on his wife.

## Chapter 5: "THE HANDWRITING'S ON THE WALL!"

*Friday, May 30th, 2014*

Anyway, we haven't talked since Tuesday, 5/27, yes, after attempted sex! The handwriting's on the wall. I will not tolerate this every-few-day passive-aggressive manipulation via days of not speaking, manifesting any time I have to bring up something. Wednesday, I called Health Net and confirmed that they cover counseling. I went online and researched family counselors. Thursday, I spent a lot more time on my research and found a Christian, black, male counselor, so that Dick cannot object to not being able to relate to him. I called and made an appointment for myself for Monday, June 2nd. Since I have not talked to Dick about counseling, I can't expect to just have his participation. However, I had realized that I needed counseling months ago, because I am not coping with this farce of a marriage – where there is seldom touching and no sex; where my husband tells me the money he makes is his, not mine; where our resources of time and money are consumed at any minute by just one call from five other people; where I am on the back burner for the next five to ten years! I don't see what benefit there is to the marriage! It is supposed to be mutually advantageous. I had earlier asked myself the question, can I contend with just being <u>patronized</u> instead of loved for 5-10 years – oh yeah – with no sex! I CAN'T!!! I need a therapist! [Man, I was so naïve then! I should have said, "I need out!!!"] "Lord, I pray that our sessions will help me and save our marriage!" But I don't just want it saved for the sake of "no breakup". I need problems solved; I don't want to just cope with the problems.

*Therefore, at some point, Dick is going to have to come to sessions.* "I pray Lord that you would be in this, and move on Dick's heart, mind and health!"

"HE'S JUST NOT THAT INTO YOU!"

But these behaviors that I want addressed are all symptomatic. It isn't going to work to just address issues each week. There are these behavioral issues because of an underlying problem. His insensitivities toward me are commensurate with how he feels about me. He <u>doesn't</u> feel for me! Thus, his behavior is consistent, and that's why he wonders why I have issues with him. Perhaps this is why he's so defensive also. Perhaps it's because I express that he's supposed to treat me like a loved wife, but he doesn't see it that way, due to his lack of passion for me. He just patronizes me – he doesn't show love to me. Again, his lack of passion towards me is congruent with his treatment. Since there is no passion, his love to me is about like that of a friend, not a wife. He might "Phileo" love me, but he is not in love with me... "Eros" love. He stopped telling me that in the early days of our marriage. I kept saying it daily, and he'd echo it, but he'd never actually say it first. "When a man tells you who he is... believe it!" Maya Angelo, who passed away two days ago, said this. He doesn't' feel love towards me, thus he doesn't say it. But if asked, he'd say he loves me. Not good enough. I married for Eros love, not just Phileo or Agape!

<u>His behavior is consistent with how he feels about me. Yet since I'm incorrectly thinking he feels more for me – like as for a wife – I'm expecting more from him than what he's able. Hence lies the dissonance! I'm speaking of how he disregards me or is insensitive towards me as a wife, but he's thinking: "I'm pretty good to my roommate... why's she trippin'?"</u>

*Also, on yesterday, 5/29, I went to my gynecologist due to irritation. I couldn't tell whether or not it was just dry, irritated or infected. I strongly felt that it was just irritated from all the attempts two days prior on splint entry. It just* hurts. She did say it was irritated. The gynecologist was just a God-send! She was also middle aged and had a husband with ED due to meds. She had a lot to share, and it really helped me. She just stopped and talked with me as long as I needed her. Her husband also had to use the "splint" method to try to insert the head. But I had to remind myself that there's a difference between her situation and mine, where my husband had failed to disclose from the beginning that he had ED. I was defrauded; she wasn't.

## "THE MIRROR HAS TWO FACES!"

### June 2nd, 2014

Well, we had a kid-free weekend, yet we had nothing planned and he was still ignoring me, so it felt like such a wasted weekend for us connecting. "Our-weekends" are too rare for us to waste them, but he's still mad about the issues I had brought up Tuesday. On Saturday, 5/31, I had been in the family room flipping back and forth between movies when he came in and sat down. I told him that I was flipping. A movie had just begun that I took note of, "The Mirror has Two Faces," with Barbara Streisand and Jeff Bridges. When it got to the premise, I realized that there were great similarities between their situation and ours. I told him that I see parallels with our relationship and that I'd like to see how this movie plays out; so we kept it on. Their situation was that he wanted a wife/roommate with whom he had no attraction, but had very similar interests; especially similar intellects. He said he wanted it platonic, but that he'd supply sex occasionally if she wanted. She actually agreed to this since she felt homely and unwanted.

The night before he was to leave for three months on business, she made an appointment for sex. He said he'd oblige her, but couldn't go through with it, and she was devastated. He rejected her, not based on looks, but on the fact that he didn't want to be turned on by his wife. Boy are the parallels mounting!

I used this opportunity to state to him that it feels very much like we're just roommates also, and that though he may love me, maybe he's not "in love" with me. I asked him if he was. He said he was. I asked how he knew. He answered, "Because I don't want to see you leave," and another few ambiguous statements. I said that these answers sounded like they could be applied to other types of relationships, but not to a spouse. They were the kinds of things I'd say to a church member who told me they were thinking about leaving the church! I believe he agreed with me, according to the, "You got me!" look on his face, and he had nothing else to say!

As the movie progressed, we'd make comments on it. He kept saying that there's something going on with the character that makes him not want sex. I think Dick was strongly relating to this man, though he said he didn't know what his issue was. On occasional commercials, I'd try to open dialogue, and when the movie was over, we had moved closer to real dialogue. I told him that I was having a real hard time being in a sexless relationship. I said that being quasi-intimate only twice a month just isn't enough for me, and that I want intimacy at least three times a week (I'm making an appointment like Barbara had to do)! Then I talked about the fact that intimacy for us is without intercourse, and of course that's a problem too. After a while, he said, well, we can't do anything sitting here. Well I took that cue and went to the bedroom.

I fondled his nipples like I usually do, because he's said from the beginning that he needs it for stimulation. Barely five minutes had passed, and I noticed something on my leg that had been draped over his body. I felt, and there was the first somewhat erection he'd ever had with me!!!!! It was trying to elongate and stiffen! He wasn't making a move for it though, so I said, "Put it in!" He climbed on top and was able to insert the head with his fingers, but without using his fingers as splints. But there wasn't much more of an erection to work with. After that, he turned me over and tried it doggy style, but couldn't. I tried to stimulate him again, but it didn't happen again. I tried in the morning too, to no avail. We briefly talked about the fact that he had taken Viagra before the movie was over, and it took a few hours to work with brief stimulation. He added, "And it wasn't Barbara Streisand!"

Well, maybe it wasn't her, but I believe it was prompted by my comments which were prompted by the movie. I stated that I saw direct parallels, and he knew that the movie was about a platonic marriage, which put him on notice! He knew that I was evaluating our future. In fact, his first response to my question, "How do you know you are still in love with me?" was, "I know because I know I don't want you to leave!" That was very telling. The fact that he was telling me that he knew we were on shaky ground – due to his ways of treating me, plus having no sex life – led him to conclude that there was perhaps not enough to keep me! I believe he panicked and decided to "break me off some"! Because why was he never able to achieve partial stiffening with the Viagra before, but this time, he had a response within five minutes of stimulation? Did he really think once was enough?

Yeah, he really does have "two faces"! This shows his manipulation and willingness to cheat me out of marital relations! He ran and got the Viagra during the movie that exposed him, because he wanted to try to produce an erection to keep me. So, his will does play a part in how Viagra works. But he had been given the samples two months prior, and never produced any degree of erection or enough elongation because he never had the will. Though he claimed to have had erections at 3 am, I know that this is entirely untrue, because after many, many, many months of a sexless marriage, any man would wake his wife up to consummate the marriage! But he claimed he was just being considerate in letting me sleep! Right!

Well, I had thought that we had turned over a new leaf! I thought that finally, we can work towards a sex life going forward – that is, if he'll take the pill and use his will! He promised an encore Sunday night, but we had gone to First-Sundays Chicago Steppin', and he was tired and had to get rest for work the next day, so he said, "The next day." BTW, we were really acting in love while steppin'. And, he actually complimented me that night as we were getting in the car, not later!

June 3rd, 2014

Monday, June 2nd, I saw the therapist for the first time. It really was the right thing to do. Even though we'd had our first quasi-sexual encounter two days before, I still knew that all the other issues were too big to be solved by one night of intimacy. Initially, I was going to concentrate on discussing the lack of sex in the relationship, but that looked like it was about to change [Naïve again!], so I talked about the other huge hurdles. By then, my journal was so extensive that I just read from it.

## MORE DECEIT

Last night, Dick and I went to Rev. class ["Revelation" Bible study at a community center]. It was the day before bills were due, so on the way there I brought up the extras that needed to be paid; reminding him that he had foregone last month's extras also. I had tried to have this discussion Sunday after church, but he just brushed me off (just didn't respond) like he does every time bills are due. He said he couldn't pay them, because he had to pay for his son's summer school. I told him that was his excuse last month, thus it couldn't be an excuse this month also! I guess he realized this, so then he said that all he'd give towards the extras was $600! Well, he knew that last month's extras included his $650 tires; the month before, our $733 hotel booking; and then I'd told him this month's extras from our vacay were $851!

I told him I knew that after paying his $1,200 plus $600 extra, plus his own bills, that he had $1,200 left! He denied it. I confirmed that his take home pay was the same, and I told him it was simple math! He tried to make me believe I didn't know what I was talking about. I asked him what he had done with the balance last month. He said he paid more on his attorney fee (from his prior divorce). When I asked how much more, he said $200 more. Well, that still leaves $1k! He never would tell me what became of that $1k!

We just can't seem to get off that merry-go-round! When we have that rare occurrence of unity, the 1$^{st}$ of the month rolls around when we have to talk financials, and the unity blows up in my face! He won't take financial responsibility, and he even uses deceit!

## MORE INSENSITIVITY

This put us at odds again; hence I was subject again to his passive-aggressive disregard. When class was over and we had only three minutes to be out of the room, I said, "We've gotta go." We started leaving, and I was out the door before I realized that he had stopped to talk to another guy. He didn't say "Hold on hun," or anything. He just carried on as though I weren't waiting. He wouldn't even acknowledge my presence, although the man he was talking to did. The other guy seemed very aware of holding me up and actually made the comment, that he didn't want to have me standing outside waiting, so he'd catch him later. It occurred to me that this is what Dick should have said! He should have been as considerate about his wife as that man was to me! I mentioned it on the way out, and Dick's response was that he didn't want to be rude to him. I said, "And so that made you rude to me!" I write this, because there are small instances, where it registers with me in that instance, that Dick just isn't into me as his wife. A husband protects his wife, in big and little things. Hopefully there are few big things, so it is the small things that count. And when those small things are forfeited, they are noticed by the perceiving wife, and they add up. In fact, they line up, with the true sentiment of his heart, which in our case is - just roommates.

Just to name a few of these instances where I picked up on Dick's insensitivity towards covering his wife: I noticed several times while on our layovers, when I'd leave my carry-on with him to use the ladies' room, when I'd return, there'd be someone sitting in my seat! I couldn't understand why he wouldn't just tell the people the seat was occupied. I did this for him each time someone wanted to sit in his seat when he went! Yes, he probably thought "she can just find another seat." Well I could have thought that too, but I didn't! Also, there was a time before we were married, that a person who owed me money was fussing at me and trying to keep the money, and I noticed that he didn't say a word in my defense. Times when his kids are over, he has fixed breakfast for his daughter, but not me, even though I was up. Also, I've been in the bedroom waiting on dinner that he was cooking for them, and I'd hear all these chairs being pulled out to sit and eat, yet he would not call me for dinner. There were many other instances of insensitivity also.

## SWALLOW "THE PILL" WITH A TALL GLASS OF "WILL"!

On last night, June 2$^{nd}$, he held to his "next day" promise, by taking Viagra right after we returned from class. Then he proceeded to lie on his back, closed his eyes and left me to do all the work! I started by fondling his nipples, and he said that tickled. So I fondled his penis for at least 15 minutes straight. He was falling in and out of sleep! He never got an erection or any elongation of course, because he took "the pill", but not the "will"! Why? Because earlier that night I had the audacity to ask him to pay bills! He never attempted to participate in the "interaction". It was as though he were saying, "If you want it, came and get it... if you can! I did my part... I took the blue pill!"

I stopped and rolled over and tried to fall asleep. This isn't the first time he's done this; I told him back then that it was very humiliating! There were times in April and May when I'd ask him to proactively take the pill to initiate sex, and he'd respond that it doesn't just "kick in". He'd say that he needs stimulation and that "It takes two to tango!" Well, several times, he refused to "tango"; he just took the pill then lay there for me to get what I can (nothing), which is humiliating!

Actually, there have been only a few times he's taken Viagra since he first got the samples on April 1st. The first time, we stood at the foot of the bed kissing, and yes, it seemed that he wasn't into it. But we kept on, and his penis started to elongate, but didn't become erect. I didn't know if that was it, or if it would keep on going. When we finally did get in bed we attempted intercourse. We probably should have kept up the stimulation, because it wasn't stiff enough to enter. The second time, absolutely nothing happened.

He had made a follow up appointment with the urologist at the beginning of May and got more samples at double the dose and an Rx. He never got the Rx filled, but cut the samples in half; so he had six to work with. But it has been exactly two months now, from the 1st samples, and there were barely three times that he's tried to have sex with me. Some of those times, he did the "lie flat and let her come get it" routine! If he used the others, he never engaged me.

For a while since having these samples, he didn't initiate sex nor tell me that he had even taken them, so I didn't know what had happened to them. Later he said he'd taken them multiple times, and they worked at 3 am! If this really happened, it was very disappointing to have missed it; yet I wonder if it really was erections, or just a little elongation. Again, he wasn't making sense in saying that it's not a magic pill and that there needs to be stimulation. So I asked, if that's the case, why he didn't initiate something before going to sleep, so that I could stimulate him so that it might work. Plus, if he really did have erections at 3 am, that was in the absence of stimulation! So either way, the truth is not being told! And finally, wouldn't you think that if an impotent man finally has his first erection of his marriage while his wife is asleep, he'd wake her up to finally consummate his marriage?

This [June 2$^{nd}$] interaction was very pivotal. Coming on the heels of his first quasi-erection [on May 31$^{st}$], I did expect things to improve; after all, I saw that Viagra works for him partially, and fast! BUT – hold your horses Janice! That night showed me that it <u>works when he wants to – work it; when he wants to control me!</u> When he is willing to participate, then it somewhat works. But mostly he is just taking it so that I can't claim that he doesn't. Those times he just doesn't participate in foreplay so as to control the lack of any outcome. As he said, "It takes two to tango!" When he chooses to "sit out" the tango, then no one dances! Again, it is CONTROL! He is a manipulator! But why? Because he really doesn't want to have sex. He's just like that guy in the movie. Not that the guy was a manipulator; at least he stated up front what the relationship would be. He did not defraud his wife. Yes, the guy had a problem, but it wasn't control and fraud. But it is apparent that Dick's problems are! I need to figure out why.

And yes, Dick <u>did</u> defraud me! He knew of his problem and hence was proceeding into a sexless marriage, but didn't get my consent in that! If my vagina were sown shut, but I didn't tell my husband before marriage, that would be fraud! And no one would expect the husband to stay and put up with it! Well that happened to me, yet I stayed, assuming that he'd medically address the problem once insured.

## PHASE 2 – SEPARATION SOLUTION!

### Chapter 6: THROUGH JUNE GLOOM TO JUNE BLOOM!

Tuesday, June 3rd, 2014

As usual, on the day that bills are due, he left a check on the nightstand for me before leaving for work. He resists giving me the check days prior when I ask. He has to be in control and wait until the last moment before he's out the door that last day! Plus, he won't give me the satisfaction of handing it to me. What is this? I know it means something! Then I noticed that it was dated the prior day, and it had a crease in it! He had written it the day before and had stuck it in his wallet or pocket; he was carrying it around instead of giving it to me! He has real issues!

We hugged hello upon his return that evening and had a little conversation about him having voted that morning [statewide primary]. We ate, and when he returned from the gym, he came in the family room where I was and kissed me, open-mouthed. This was the first open-mouthed kiss I'd had from him in a very long time.

It was reminiscent of our pre-marriage days, not only because it was open-mouthed, but because it was very sticky like I remembered from back when we were dating and kissed open-mouthed. Since he stopped kissing me after we were married, I had forgotten all about the sticky residue from his mouth.

This reminds me of the fact that once we got married, he started kissing me with pursed lips instead of open-mouthed, and I'd tell him that I missed our kissing. He'd just laugh it off. Again, he was controlling the intimacy in our relationship.

Then he came and sat with me as I watched TV. We used to watch "The Haves and the Have Nots" together, so I thought we were about to reignite our old pre-marital routine. Then, at 9:30, he gets a phone call, answers it and then goes out of the room. I know that it's his ex. She calls several times a week, but normally during dinner time! I fully expected him to end the conversation quickly and come right back. It was late, plus we finally had a little "us-time"; we were finally getting our groove back! I actually thought this would be important enough for him to tell his "ex" that he was with his "next", and he'd have to go. Not!

He stayed on the phone a very long time! When the show was over, I went to the room where he was, and he didn't acknowledge me, though he knew I was there. He just kept talking in a sweet tone, and I thought, well maybe his ex had handed the phone to Jill, and that's why he was speaking in such a sweet tone in my presence! So I returned to the TV and waited. I went back maybe 20 minutes later and decided to just stand there and catch his attention. I heard him saying, "Jack is on his way off to school and has done well, Jane too, and Jill is doing all right..." I therefore knew it wasn't any of his kids he was speaking to! I caught his eye enough for him to know it was time to end it, and then I went to the bedroom. He came in after about five more minutes of talking and then told me it was his ex. He immediately went into why she called and why it took so long. He said she had just returned from her therapist regarding some unresolved issues, and at his prompting, was reaching out to those with whom she needed to talk these issues through! My eyes were just wide open, not knowing where to begin.

[What is it about this man that sends his wives to therapists?!!!!!!!]

I said, "So she calls a married man at 9:30 pm and keeps him on the phone for an hour!" He said, well she had just left her therapist! I asked several other warranted questions, and he had a quick defense of her for each! I asked how it was that he was speaking so sweetly to her. He said she was going through things, and he was helping her!

Before this escalated, I spring boarded onto the therapy issue. I asked had they gotten counseling when they were going through. He said no, things were too far gone. I asked what about before they were too far gone. He said she wanted to, but he didn't. I asked, even to save his marriage, wasn't he willing to get counseling? He said "No." My eyes are getting wider! I decided that was the time to ask if he was willing for us to go to counseling to save our marriage. He said, "Yes." I was relieved. I told him that I had already seen a counselor the day before, and that I'd really like for us to go as a couple, and that I felt that our issues could be resolved.

I was emboldened to say something I've been rehearsing to say for months. I've said it in many different and milder ways all this year, but he always brushed me off or got defensive. I went ahead and directly said that there were two things that I needed him to do. I told him that they are both phone calls that I need him to make tomorrow. I went on to say they were very important to me, because these issues affect us both, not just him. He cuts me off with that impatience I've been seeing more of lately and says, "Just tell me what it is. I don't need all this other stuff!" I said I needed to preface it, because he gets so defensive every time I bring it up and says it's his business, not mine. I said I need him to make two appointments tomorrow: one with his primary care doc, and one with CSS [Child Support Services] to address the $77k arrears bill which he technically does not owe.

[Isn't it something that I have to rehearse what I'm going to say to my own husband? But I knew how he jumps defensive so fast, so I tried to find the best way to present issues!]

He defensively said, "I've already done that!" I was relieved, and in that moment, I really thought, "Wow, those were two of the biggies as far as our issues are concerned, so if he addresses them completely, we could be well on our way to making the marriage work!" Boy was I naive! I expressed how relieved I was that he had done this and asked why he hadn't told me, since I've been asking all year! He said "It was my business, not yours; I don't have to tell you things! Who are you to think I have to tell you things? Who are you to make demands of me?" It turned nasty fast! I couldn't believe that night! First, I have to contend with him giving his ex an hour of "our-time", talking sweetly to her, and then him turning on me for making a request – expressing concern for his health and our finances! I know it is human nature for some to try to turn the tables when they themselves are guilty. He knew he was inappropriate with his ex, and now he is displacing the guilt with another subject!

*Moving on, since I did not expect him to say that he'd made the calls, I asked if he had expressed the fact [to CSS] that he was unemployed for the period of billing. This was when he went off on me! He really let me have it; his angry response was sooooooooo unusual and unnecessary that, again, I think he was trying to distract me from his loving conversation with his ex! He said things like, "Who do you think I am? I'm a man! I know how to make a request! You don't have a right to ask me all these questions!" I immediately stood up for myself and said "Do not talk to me that way!" He kept on, and I said "I won't allow you to talk to me that way!" He said, "And I won't allow you to talk to me that way!" I asked "What way?" He said, "Questioning me! I know how to take care of business!" I said, "This is business you should have taken care of five months ago when they garnished more wages than they should have; that doesn't reflect taking care of business!" He kept hollering and wagging his head back and forth. I then pointed out how sweet he had been to his ex just moments ago, but now look at how he talks to his wife! He said, "Well, at least she doesn't question me!" How hurtful – that he'd defend his ex-wife while putting me down! He kept up the act for a while, getting louder and nastier, and I again stated that I would not allow him to go on speaking to me that way. He is a "tit for tat" kinda guy, so he stated the same. Again, I asked, "What had I said? What have I done to you?" I said, "You've never, once, ever in our marriage told me what you have against me. Tell me what you have against me!" He refused to. He just said, "We'll just get this straightened out in counseling!" I asked why he wouldn't tell me what I've* ever done to him, but he couldn't come up with a thing. All he said was that every time he tries to bring something up, I take it the wrong way. I told him he's never brought up anything that I've done or said to him that was hurtful, so he'd have no way of knowing how I'd react. Since he was now telling lies, I realized it could go nowhere; once more I stated that it really hurts that he could talk to his ex so sweetly, but all he has for me is hollering. He said, "Well I was 'ministering' to her!" On the way out, I said, "Well I wish you'd 'minister' to me!"

The man defended his ex against his wife! Lord knows, each time I've typed "ex", I had stopped myself from typing "wife", because I really do feel like, "positionally", she is still his wife!

I realized another reason for his defensiveness regarding the arrears assessment of child support. He had never reported to CSS years ago the fact that he had become unemployed, so they continued their assessment of child support, although there was no way to garnish it. Hence they assessed him $11k arrears child support for the period when there was no wage garnishment. He again contended that he's been in the "system" for 20 years, so he knows how to work it. I said if he truly knew the system, he would have known to submit a form when he lost his job 2 ½ years ago, and they would have adjusted his child support assessment then and we wouldn't owe $11k now! I said he also would have known that they'd come after him once he was employed.

In fact, I had made it a point before we got married to ask him if he was responsible for child support for his period of unemployment, and he point blank told me "No!" Well he was wrong! But even at this point, they still would have investigated a late claim and perhaps lowered his arrears assessment. Why not try to save us thousands of dollars? BTW, he flip-flopped again on how much arrears he's paying. Months ago he said it was $200 monthly. On 5/27 he said it was $800, now he says it's $120. He is able to read a statement, so I know what's really going on! He's being intentionally deceptive!

### "WHEN A WOMAN'S FED UP...!"

Friday, June 6th, 2014

Again, he hasn't talked to me since Tuesday night. Wednesday and Thursday morning he didn't peck-kiss me goodbye, which is typical for his "non-speaking" days. This has been an ugly and childish pattern. A wife should be able to bring up issues to her husband for resolution without him getting defensive, nasty, then silent and unaffectionate for days on end! I'm simply fed up and want no part of him anymore if this is his M.O.! For the first time, I woke up cursing him in my head. This is a bad sign.

## FAMILY MATTERS

Okay, so today he did peck-kiss me before leaving. He called from work saying he'd be home at 9 pm because he was picking Jack up from the Greyhound station late, then going to get the rest of the kids. He's planning to take them to his parents' home Saturday, while he and his dad take care of some biz. This all works for me because I'm conditioned to expect to be disregarded those weekends. Those weekends are defined by his ignoring me, some of the kids not even acknowledging me, and everyone lying around the entire weekend watching TV instead of interacting as a family. It's like I'm just running a hotel, or like he's saying, "Don't mind her; she just lives here!" Initially when they first come in, sometimes they speak... sometimes not. I make sure that we have good interaction at the dinner table, but otherwise, I'm not acknowledged. And when the TV is playing loudly, or worse, when they spread out to both the living room and family room to watch our only two TVs (which then confines me to my room), I just need relief! So I do look forward to the times that the schedule is different, breaking the TV marathon routine.

## FAMILY MATTERS HAVE ROOTS!

Saturday, June 7$^{th}$, 2014

Last night, Dick got in at 9 pm with the kids and chicken dinners. We all talked at the dinner table, but he and I didn't afterward. He sent them to bed right afterwards and proceeded to watch TV in the living room while I was in the *family room. I watched a little TV and then I went to bed. The next morning he hugged me before he and the kids left to go to his parents' home and run errands with his dad.*

While at a church meeting this morning, I kept thinking about us. Thoughts kept unfolding... new revelations. I kept thinking about his quick defensiveness and how in our last conversation, he kept saying things like, "I'm a man!", and "Don't you think I know how to take care of business?" Real strange comments... but they have a root. He has felt emasculated in the past! We don't have enough history for it to be me; he has jumped defensive from our first argument. And when I say argument, I mean my bringing up a valid concern in a nice manner and his cutting me like a knife with defensive and attacking comments. Then I respond to the attack, not the real issue... which gets buried.

He clearly came into this marriage with this complex. I thought it was his ex that he was used to reacting like that to, but perhaps it is his mom. If there was any red flag that I saw going into this marriage, it was the way that he spoke to his mom on the phone.

*From the beginning of our dating, when I'd hear him answer the phone, he'd answer, "What?", then continue being real short and disrespectful. I'd hear a woman's voice and think it was his ex. When I finally found out it was his mom, I was floored! This went on repeatedly, and I asked him about it. He answered, "Well, she's always calling asking me if I did this or that!" (Concerning his job hunt.) Well, his parents were supporting him, so I think they had a right to see if he was actively looking for work after over a year of unemployment! I'd keep hearing this tone, and sometimes I'd bring it up again, and he'd say, "Well she keeps calling with advice, and if she forgets something, she'll call right back!" Incidentally, I noticed that the calls that actually were from his ex were very civil... even friendly.*

*They say that the way a man treats is mom is the way he'll treat his wife. I realized that this could come bite me in our marriage, so I needed to address this. One day I told him of my concern over the way he speaks to his mother. He listened like he was taking it in, and I never heard him speak to his mom in that tone again! I thought that the problem was solved before our marriage! Early in our marriage, there were times I saw responses to me that made me think he was responding as to his mom - not too harsh, but yet noticeable. I remember thinking, "He's just going to have to give me a pass! I'm not his mom, and he can't displace on me!" I didn't speak it though because I thought it might make him more defensive. Well, it didn't take long in our marriage, until he was outright defensive at everything I'd say. It could be as simple as, "Baby, do you mind using some mouthwash; I'm smelling your breath." His response was always, "Well I don't smell it! I'd be the first to smell my own breath!" This is ludicrous! There's a whole mouthwash industry out there because everyone's breath stinks at some point! I would really appreciate it if someone, especially my husband, would alert me if my breath were offensive. I'd thank him and immediately rinse! Sometimes when we're driving somewhere, I have to keep my head turned to the right to avoid catching that odor. Sometimes it fills up the whole car!*

*I have learned that I can't say anything to him about any issue that needs attention. But some issues need addressing, so I actually rehearse them in my mind, to make sure nothing can be misconstrued and taken defensively. Well, they always are! And sometimes he doesn't let me finish a thought* before his defensive response, so even my rehearsed lines don't make it to the end! I shouldn't have to rehearse what I'm going to say to my husband. I'm walking on eggshells very early in our marriage!

Back to his relationship with his parents; here are other things I've noticed. He was reluctant to tell his parents that he was getting married! I think it was his mom with whom he was reticent.

We got engaged July 27$^{th}$, 2013. Week after week, he said he'd tell her, but didn't. He even saw his parents in person a few times, but didn't. He told his kids though. Our wedding date was to be September 19$^{th}$, 2013, so I kept insisting that he tell her sooner than later, but he held off. Finally, I said I wanted to have them over for Labor Day, and that he needed to tell them then. He finally did! This gave his mom very little time (2½ weeks) to get used to the idea. Is this why it seems that she hasn't fully accepted me?

There have been times, since we've been married, that she has invited him over, but says she doesn't want a whole lot of people in her house... meaning me. She is very nice to me when I'm invited though, and I like her very much; it's just that sometimes I'm not invited!

Also, he seems to take on a different, childlike persona when in their company. He probably is unaware that (sometimes) he strikes a defensive pose – like he's just waiting for them to say something to which to object. Sometimes he doesn't look right at them when talking and is kind of sarcastic and *short with his responses; kind of like a teenaged boy would do. I thought it was just his mom, but it is even with his dad. Dick has a dependent relationship with his parents (again, like a teen), yet he still kind of snaps responses to them, not showing appreciation (as a man would). I think he resents his dependence on them. His dad wrote checks to him the months he was unemployed, and unbeknownst to me, even once he got the job last May. (I found out that his dad still paid his rent until we got married!) A couple times since our marriage he has asked his dad for money; even a few weeks ago when his eldest son's summer school fee came up. Now here's a contradiction: he asked his dad for this money even though he told me he couldn't pay our hotel or new tire bill due to his "allegedly" paying it himself! What a liar!*

I see that he is still in a sort of childlike dependence with his parents, and this dysfunction itself is cause for his projecting on me, resulting in lashing out and defensiveness. Teens go through a period where they are extremely defensive, and I believe he sees himself as still in that state with his parents, but he projects it to our circumstances. He has made me his mother in his mind, and he is struggling for his independence – something he should have had already – long before he proposed to me!

*I also notice that he refers to the monetary gifts as from his dad, not his parents. This has always stuck with me. Why does he not see it as their money? Well, when I was at his parents' home for Memorial Day, I recall a conversation with his dad about their house that he had built decades ago, where he responded, "Well, it was my money! I can do what I want with my money!"*

Wow! Is this where Dick gets it from? I don't know if this was an arrangement that his parents had agreed upon, but Dick can't project their arrangement onto our household! And even if his dad did think this way, he had no financial obligations elsewhere, so he spent "his" money at, and on his home with his wife! But in my case, my husband's money went out to his other households, and our household got the leftovers!

So, it seems that both father and son believe their income belongs to them alone. And if perhaps all these years that really was his dad's position, then perhaps this is why I've heard his mom respond to his dad with boundary statements. So in essence, Dick is thinking like him and retorting like her. But Dick's dad is very mellow and doesn't attack or say anything remotely negative; in fact he tends to back off and yield to her. I believe Dick picks up on this and determines he's not going to become a husband who yields. Hence, Dick has it triple-bad! He thinks the money is his; he speaks defensively like her, using his own set of boundary statements like, "I'm not going to stand for it!", and then he becomes passive-aggressive as a stance! Wow! No wonder I'm going through so much! And then, add to it Dick's shame of ED on top of that! God help me!

All this points to his issues with his relationships/interactions with women. They have either been his mama or baby-mama. He has had no close relationship with a woman who isn't either his mama or his baby-mama. Since I am neither, I am an anomaly to him, and he hadn't learned where to place me. Before, he treated me very well, but once married, in his subconscious, he had to reconcile how to relate to a woman who isn't his mama, isn't his baby-mama, but who expects to be his lover. That is because, prior to our marriage, sex wasn't an issue; sex wasn't expected, so his ED wasn't a factor. Once sex became a factor, he couldn't reconcile it. When (as a wife) I bring up relational issues, he reacts to me like I'm his mom instead of his wife. In fact, he talks to me the way I used to hear him talk to his mother when we were dating. And this explains why his reactions to me are so immature! He always sounded like a child, saying very unreasonable things. Well, he was playing the role of the resistant teenager towards his mother. Now, the interesting contrast is that when his baby-mama brings up something, then he is able to respond to her nicely, because he has "owned up" to his "dad" role for her household! I don't have the place in his heart of mama or baby-mama, and because he doesn't relate sexually, he can't relate to me as his wife... so I have no real place in his life. He can't own up to the full husband role.

To put it another way, before marriage, he showed lots of attention and affection, which is a natural response to the way we felt about each other. Since sex was ruled out from the beginning due to our choice of celibacy, he could feel natural in his expressions towards me. Sex was not the end; it was not expected. Once married and sex was expected, then he backed off of the attention and affection that could lead to sex. As a married man, Dick is perfectly happy spooning. He used to smile from ear to ear when we were about to spoon. But as time went on, I believe he had to distance himself from me to keep us from intimate times that might lead me to want more of him than he could give.

[Wow, didn't I just break it down?!! But this was all revelation through the Holy Spirit! I began this section by saying that I was pondering issues while at a meeting. My disgusting marriage was distracting me while I was supposed to be meeting with others, so the best thing for me to do was to journal when I returned home. Once I did that, my questions were answered through the Holy Spirit just downloading revelation as I journaled! It is cathartic and progressive towards a resolution.]

## REVELATIONS THROUGH MOVIES

*I've been catching a lot of movies lately that seem to speak to my circumstances. "The Mirror Has Two Faces"; "Why Did I Get Married"; "Newlywed" (couples found that their marriages were unofficial, so they evaluated if they should move forward or not); "Something Borrowed" (a couple that seemed meant for each other); "Second Honeymoon" (a couple contemplating divorce wins a dream honeymoon). When viewing "Premonition", I had even forgotten that I had seen it before, because I saw it this time from the perspective of a hurting wife. In the first scene where both the husband and wife were about to speak, I would have thought that when he turned to see her, he'd have a look of love in his eye. But immediately I picked up on the blank look... the same look I* get from Dick! No caring, no interest! Immediately, I knew that they had marital issues and that they were just co-existing! This was confirmed when she told a friend that they were just roommates. He kept pulling away from her and distancing himself because he had something to hide. I saw a lot of things in these movies to which I could now relate and now make relationship re-evaluations.

STILL IN LAST PLACE...

June 11$^{th}$, 2014

On Sunday, 6/8, when I returned from the gym, I expected to watch Columbo as I do on Sunday nights. Dick was in the kitchen, and his three kids were watching something in the family room. I told Dick that I had planned on watching Columbo, which is only available through the cable box in the family room, so he said he'd turn. He sat down with the remote trying to find it, so when I came in, all the seats were taken. He didn't ask any of his kids to let me have a seat, and he had already made it clear to me that I was not to ask his kids to do anything. Again, I felt left out; so I left out. I sat in my room, and when he came to me later, I asked him where he expected me to sit. He said he would have gotten up. Well, there was no way for me to know this; all I knew was what was happening then. He didn't offer a seat; his kids didn't either, so once again, I felt left out. He said, "It's not like I was taking over!" I replied that the room was taken over, but no one offered a seat. He said, "Then I'll empty the room!"

This comment was very indicative of his "separate households" mentality. I wanted to sit in there with them as a family and watch my show, but there was no seat. He'd rather empty the room than have his kids share it with me.

*This is noteworthy because it isn't the first time that Dick has done nothing when both TVs were unavailable to me. The problem really lies in the fact that he won't remind the kids of the arrangement. The other problem with this is that he won't insist that they speak when I come in there. Whenever I come in, I speak, but they won't look up from TV and speak, and I feel that is very rude. I've asked Dick to instruct them to speak, and he's only done that once. Do some parenting, Dick, especially since you won't let me! So due to Dick not looking out for me, not only do I feel displaced, but I feel disrespected. So, it's not the kids. They're great kids; it's just Dick's insensitivity towards me.*

This is really the issue, not the TV. I don't even watch that much TV. These incidents are just fuel to the fire of feeling last and left out in his world, because he won't consider me in even little things. It is just another thing that puts me in my place... last place. And I'm resisting it, but to no avail. He should try to unite us and make sure that I'm regarded, but he won't.

I wish that we could have united activities. But his kids like to watch kid shows all day, and I don't. I prefer to listen to the music channel than to watch any TV. But the main reason is that Dick has already set up two different households due to his wearing his "daddy only" hat when they're here. Thus, this already sets me up as the outsider. Then add to that, feelings of disrespect, and literal displacement! Having the agreement to have the kids use the living room TV solves the problem of displacement. I've tried to solve the disrespect issue, but Dick hardly speaks himself when I come in, so how can I expect him to have them speak? I've talked to him about the "hat" problem and ways to connect so that I see the "husband hat" too, but he's only done this twice in over eight months.

But it isn't just the lack of unity of activities. It is the lack of unity of families in his mind. Everything he does and says puts his family with his kids above his insignificant family with his wife. This is evident from his instruction that I am not to tell his kids what to do. I can't even tell them to clean up behind themselves, and he won't either. This played out even to the smallest detail.

*For instance, since I can't ask them to clean up after themselves when they would leave crumbs on the couches and floors, I'd asked Dick to limit their eating to the kitchen table; they're not to eat in the living room or family room anymore. He agreed. Then he also agreed that I wouldn't have to clean up after them at the table anymore; that he'd have them clean up the crumbs in their chairs and on the table, and that he'd have them take turns sweeping the floor around them. That never happened! I still clean up after them!*

*And another instance that showed me he didn't want me to ask them to do work was one day when we had company over. I was running behind, so I asked him to come in the kitchen and help me, but he kept acting like he didn't hear me. So then I asked his kids for help, and they came in. I gave them tablecloths to put on the two tables on the patio. They went out to do it, at which time, Dick ran to me asking, "What did you ask my kids to do?" When I told him, he went out there, took the cloths from them, and did it himself! This was a clear message to me as well as to the kids, that they're not to take any direction from me!*

Another instance of them knowing that they don't have to follow my rules is that he lets them eat in the living room and family room, even though he told me he wouldn't let them. He claims that they're being supervised! Twice, I've even caught them sneaking food in the living room and hiding it when I come in! This is not their fault, but his, because they know that he disregards our agreements and lets them disregard my rules. Yes, we are two separate households, and I am totally disregarded!

Dick also shows them that I'm to be disregarded concerning my request that they not waste the food on their plates. I ask them to get what they'll eat and eat what they get. This is even objectionable to Dick. When I see them wasting food and I ask them to finish it, Dick would be right there, picking up their plates and putting the leftovers in the fridge; in essence, rescuing them and intimating that they don't have to do as I said! And of course I know that they're not coming back to that food! And certainly not when they return in two weeks! Yet Dick has left their leftovers in there many weeks... as if that placated me. It only let me (and them) know that my word carried no weight when it comes to his kids.

## HARAMBEE! LET'S COME TOGETHER!

However, this is not to say that I haven't tried to unite the two households. First of all, I had planned to do the cooking the weekends his kids came, because I went into this seeing us as one household, not two. So I recall the first weekend that they were here; I had cooked chicken Cacciatore, and I had "put my foot in it!" But they proceeded to pick everything out, including my foot! So I realized that they're picky eaters, and that Dick should do the cooking those weekends; he knows their taste.

To unite us, many times I've said, "Let's do something other than watch TV. Let's get out and play some tennis, or go for a drive." We never did. The kids just wanted to watch TV, and Dick always conceded to this. Additionally, I was the initiator of the only two times that we ever did something different, which was to play trivia in the family room. He was even reluctant about that. He said, "They might not want to." I said, "Well, you don't ask them if they want to; of course teens will say no. You just say, 'When that show goes off, meet us in the family room.'" They seemed to enjoy it. But all the other times when I say that they watch TV too much, he says he wants them to, because they do so much during the week that he wants them to relax. Two of them are in sports and doing real well in school, but I still don't think that means they should lie around all weekend watching TV. [I believe he was simply trying to be the "fun dad", allowing the mom to be the functional parent; which she did very well, because their kids are really wonderful, likable, bright and well-rounded. Hats off to his ex!]

One time, I intercepted Jill on her way from the dinner table back to the TV and had her come over to the piano. I taught her some elementary things. She seemed interested, so I told her that I could teach her every time she's here. I gave her a scale fingering drill to practice at home on the table. When she came back, she said she had practiced and showed me. Then there was one Monday that she was here with me on a holiday; I taught her the basics of reading sheet music. She was very excited about learning it and seemed to want to follow up. Next time, I asked her dad to let her take a break from TV for piano lessons, and he wouldn't. He said, maybe she doesn't want to. I asked her, and she said "No." So her dad would rather his daughter not get free piano lessons twice a month because his philosophy is to let kids do what they want to do. I'm so glad that my parents didn't ask, but told me they'd made piano lesson arrangements for me when I was young. I kept up lessons until I went away to college, and it built a great sense of self-esteem in me.

This holiday when she was home with me, I also had her read as much time as she spent watching TV. She wasn't making much progress on her book, so I sat and talked with her. She said she hated reading. I talked about how it is still important and can be fun with the right book. I also noticed that she kept losing focus, so I read some with her. I showed her how to pace herself to read faster. We both read and timed ourselves and pushed our rate higher. She got the hang of it. She also shared about the grades she anticipates in some of her classes. We were bonding, and I was trying to be of assistance. But this bonding and assistance was only possible because her dad was at work. Otherwise, he would have had her watching TV instead. It's preferable for any student to spend more time in the books, and less on TV, but her father resists me every time I suggest this. It is baffling! But this goes right back to his notion of two separate households, and of course I have no say in his household with his kids.

## TOO MUCH TOO LITTLE TOO LATE – #TWO!

June 11th, 2014

Monday night/Tuesday morning, Dick reached out in bed and rubbed my hip then stomach. He spent a lot of time on my stomach, so I wasn't sure if he was trying to get sexual or not. I waited to see, and after a while I just moved his hand to my breast. He proceeded in foreplay and then attempted sex with no erection.

Tuesday morning, we did caress in bed, and he did kiss me goodbye (Monday morning as well), but there was no real interaction that evening besides general talk about the news. No touching in bed Tuesday night, and Wednesday morning he got to sleep in late due to a 9:30 am doc appt. But he didn't use that time to get busy with me; he got up and watched the news. We went to the doc appt., only to find out that Dick hadn't taken the time to check the location. His appointment was at the San Bernardino location, not Upland. He got another appt. for the next morning, 8 am. This will be his first appt. with a decent primary care physician.

*June 13th, 2014*

*On yesterday, June 12th, we went to the doc. When the nurse asked him the nature of his visit, for the first time, I heard him acknowledge the possibility of diabetes. Dick shared general things with the doc; I shared specific concerns. I gave the doc the prior lab work copies. He's to get more lab work and return on 6/25.*

*The evening was typical; lightweight to non-existent dinner conversation. He did come in the family room to read, and we ended up watching "Stomp the Yard" together. He fell asleep, and I went to bed, although I had tried to awaken him to go to bed.*

*Today is Friday, and we have no plans for the weekend. I lay in bed that night, naked and so firm from my workouts, and so soft from my moisturizing routine; I thought it was such a waste that he'd rather stay up watching TV than hug on this fine body!*

[You might be interested in this moisturizing routine: use up to a tablespoon of either olive oil or avocado pulp in your bath water. When your avocados are getting old (but before they get hard and black), just scoop out the pulp by the tablespoon and freeze it. It's great to first rub it on your heels under water (no more cracked heels), and as it breaks up, apply some to your face and let it dry as a facial mask. Let the rest continue to dissolve by swishing it around the whole tub. It makes your skin real dewy!]

Sunday, June 15th, 2014

Saturday, we existed apart again. I had extremely tight shoulders for two days, so I decided to ask him to massage them. He used to voluntarily give me very frequent rub downs when we were dating, then he stopped once married. No maintenance for a long time. He did some massaging after dinner and then said he'd continue after his shower; he had been in the pool. We sat, with me on the floor in front of him, massaging and watching TV. When done, I sat on the same couch cushion with him, yet he did not put his arm around me or touch me with his hands at all, even though our bodies were tight up against each other. I thought that was so indicative of his lack of intimacy interest, because he has to intentionally not touch, being that close.

He did continue the massage in bed this morning, however, which led to intercourse-less intimacy. It's like he doesn't know how to come on to me; he needs a crutch like a massage, even though I've told him that I desire affection and sex. He said we'd pick it up tonight, with some assistance. I asked how many "assistants" he had left. He said, three. I don't understand why; almost six weeks after getting his second Viagra samples he still has three out of six left. With our sex life being flat-lined and my telling him how I'm not coping with it, why would he sit on half his supply? In fact, he only used two involving me! The famous May 31st time, when he had some response, and two days later when he did the "come and get it if you can" number... laid out flat, eyes closed, falling in and out of sleep! You'd think that after over eight months of no intercourse when there was that one time that Viagra started to work, he'd go through the rest of his supply to try to get the same response! No; sex attempts seem to be on his terms: when he wants it, or when he can use it to try to keep me onboard.

I say this, because the only time that he actually tried, to some avail, was when I shared more of my concerns during that Barbara Streisand movie. Also, after I told him that we have an imminent counseling appointment, he made a decent attempt. Could our encounter this weekend have been due to wanting to have something positive to report to the counselor? I don't know. Maybe it's just his cycle of "breaking me off some" every two weeks! And "breaking me off some" implies just interest... not intercourse.

### CHASING THE "O" AND HICKEYS!

*Tuesday, June 17th, 2014*

Dick has kept up the interest since our last encounter. He seems to be chasing that orgasm he didn't have this weekend. Sunday night, intercourse-less sex had gone on for a long time with no climax. Even though he has no erections and no penetration, he always has an orgasm; except this time. He chased it for a good while, and even when we both woke up in the night, he tried again. I noticed him trying to put hickeys on me. But it wasn't like it was out of passion; it was like he had an objective and timeline to put a hickey on me. Then I realized the truth: he was trying to mark me in time for the therapist session the next day – so that it would appear that we had a sex life! I didn't want him to mark me for that reason, so I kept turning my head. Turns out... he did mark me.

## MIXED MESSAGES DON'T MOVE ME!

Yesterday, I saw the therapist, and that evening when Dick came home from work, he was very friendly and attentive and affectionate. We went to Rev. class, and when we got back, he washed the few dishes in the sink (nice); we caught a good show that listed the top 10 moments in Lakers history, then we went to bed. He was still showing attention and affection, so I thought we could have had a repeat! But he went to sleep. When I woke up at 7:30, he was getting ready leave for a conference at 8:00, but he came over to my side and got in bed behind me (a cool move!). I thought it would be about a minute of spooning, and it turned into 1.5 hours! Yeah, he was real late! I was really surprised, but he let the spooning go on to breast rubbing and then grinding. He never attempted sex though, and he didn't climax from the grinding. He made comments that he couldn't go because he had a naked body in bed next to him. I replied that he has had a naked body in bed next to him for nine months, yet he's never done anything like this before! In fact, last night when we were undressing for bed, he made the comment that he thinks he likes my naked body in bed! Quite a shocker, so I said something like what I said this morning. He tried to play it off by saying, "Well it was cold then, but now it's warming up, so we can enjoy it!"

Okay, please help me to decipher this! First of all, we don't have winter weather in CA! During that season, we just put an extra comforter on the bed, and if he's cold, he wears PJ's! But I'm always nude. And it didn't just get warm.

It's been warmer than it is now both late last year and earlier this season. It very much sounded like an excuse!

Back to this morning and since Sunday morning – he has been very frisky and attentive, which is what I've always dreamt of from him. So you'd think that I'd be feeling relieved and hopeful. I am not.

The fact that I'm not is very telling. I was just informing my therapist yesterday, that I am such an optimistic and hopeful person, that I do hang on to the smallest thing for hope. That has gotten me through this far. But I am spent! I have no more hope, and even this extraordinary act this morning and weekend is too much, too little, too late! I was so not moved by it that it shocked me! I could hardly recognize my inward response. Of course, my outward response was receptive, but inwardly, I had come to terms with the fact that this did not change our circumstances, and thus, I am not moved!

## THERAPIST THOUGHTS

This brings me to the point where I shall share about my visit to the therapist yesterday. I didn't bring my journal with me, and I shared about how things were status quo (meaning he was aloof and unaffectionate) until Sunday morning, when we had sexless intimacy, precipitated by a neck massage request from me. I told the doc about his statement about using Viagra to follow up that Sunday night; I also shared my thoughts about how Dick knew he possibly had the key to unlocking a sexual relationship between us, yet he sat on half of his supply! It makes me feel like he is trying to control our sex life... and me! He dishes it out only when he wants to – twice a month – and since April 1$^{st}$, when he got his first Viagra sample, he has tried them with me only four times! That's four times in two and a half months! And two of those times were the "come and get it if you can" encounters, where he lay flat and wouldn't participate!

I told the doc that I feel controlled by this behavior of "meting out sex", and I feel mistreated. He asked why I think Dick needs control. I said I didn't know why for sure... it could be tied to his ED, but I told him at this point, it doesn't matter why. At this point, I'm all fed up, I'm spent, I have nothing left, and something's gotta give! I told him I can't take it anymore. I said that this has been how I've been feeling for a while now, and his display of attention and affection Sunday is just too late! It does not sway me! He has just run out of time! And since my therapist and I had run out of time, we planned to continue on our next appointment, which was to include Dick.

Thursday, June 19th, 2014

Today, we had our nine-month wedding anniversary; even to the day. Neither of us voiced our remembrance of it! We went to bed in silence.

Saturday, June 21st, 2014

Friday, the kids didn't come due to other plans. Friday night, we watched TV in the family room, separate, and then we went to bed. Later in the night when we both stirred, he reached out and initiated sex with sucking my breasts. He didn't do much foreplay and never managed to kiss me. He quickly turned me over for "doggy" style sex, and I wondered why, because he is unsuccessful at "splinting" the head of his penis in that way. He went on a long time, fumbling, trying to get a soft penis in, and for a while, he was at the wrong place! I waited to see if he'd realize he was too far back, so finally I told him, "That's the wrong hole!" He shifted and worked a while at it, when I finally said, "You have better luck from the front." So he turned me over "froggy" style, and he was able to "splinter" the head in for our "sex-simulation." But there is no shaft for stroking, so... that's it!

Saturday morning, he was out early taking Jane back to college with his dad and son, and I went to the "Women Encouraging Women" conference [Founder, Edna Harris]. It was good. When I returned, I finalized my "Journal Conclusion" that I had been working on since my last appointment and printed it for our session Monday. [I really thought this "Journal Conclusion" would be the end of my journal, because my revelations had led me to my resolution. Boy was I wrong! This was when I began to bloom! My journey was just beginning!]

## WE'RE OFF TO SEE THE THERAPIST!

June 23rd, 2014

Today is the day that Dick and I go as a couple to see the marriage counselor. I'm looking forward to it, because we get to "push the reset button!" It's the only way that our marriage is to survive. So I'm looking forward to that which can stop our downward spiral and set us on a new course. On this journey, I look forward to regaining my friend, having the man whom I fell in love with reemerge and to find some closure to our issues. Things were so much better before we were married. And so one thing that this new arrangement [I expound later] will do is allow us to go back to our pre-marital conditions and take some time to see who we are together and to rediscover the love that was there. I hope he sees this as the opportunity that I see.

Well - signing off now. I turn the page this evening! We start a whole new chapter!!!! No turning back!!!!!! AMEN!!!!!!

### Chapter 7: WHOA! WHAT A MESS HE IS! OUR SESSION!

Tuesday, June 24th, 2014

Wow! Wow! All I can say is... WOW!!!!!! Now I know why we have so many problems!!!! All I suspected is true... and then some! If there was ever an OMG moment! Wow! But what I should really say is, TYG! "Thank you God," for revealing the truth to me!!! Thank you!!!

The therapist began, yesterday, by asking Dick to share how he met me and where we are today. He told the story, and then the doc had to ask him again about our current state of affairs. Dick couldn't think of anything! He was like, "Hum, let me see..." for such a long time. He finally said it felt like we were in a rut. He said our communication isn't like it used to be. He said he's feeling overwhelmed, but he didn't expound. He went on to say, though we like some of the same music, we have different musical tastes; his is more eclectic. He said we don't like the same movies; he likes action and adventure, and I don't. (Wow, this is so superficial and certainly not true. My favorite movies are this genre!!!) He just couldn't come up with anything of substance!!!

Doc had to prompt him to say more... to go deeper. He asked about the relating. After searching for something, Dick said, "Well, I'm no Denzell!" Doc and I had the same confused look. Dick said he doesn't look like he used to. He said that in the past, he didn't have to chase girls; they came to him. Dick said he is not the "Alpha Male." When the doc sought clarification, Dick said he is not like the "cave man", grabbing his woman and pulling her in and having his way with her. He doesn't do the pursuing/initiating. Wow! I was confused! Doc said, "So as roles go, if you're not the hunter, then you're the gatherer?" Dick said, "Yes." Doc said, then you kind of take on the female role, and if she takes on the female role too, then we have a problem. I could see that Dick realized the dilemma.

Dick still wouldn't ID any specific marital issue, so the doc asked him if everything is fine in the bedroom, and Dick said "Yes"!!!! He asked if everything was working the way you both would like. Dick really wasn't going to discuss his ED... like I wasn't going to! He said, "Well Janice seems to think it could be better!" Without mentioning the ED, he talked about going to the doc and having elevated levels, and that he's trying to watch his eating. He said, "Well, I'm not 17 anymore; it doesn't just rise when the wind blows anymore!" Wow! He is really in denial. He was dancing around the ED issue.

He also said "It takes two!" meaning that I need to stimulate him. He also said that I put expectations on him, and if it doesn't rise in five minutes, I roll over and stop. Very much a lie! I have actually looked at the clock after our encounters because we rub and grind for so long that I actually wanted to see how long. Most of the time, it's close to an hour. I've even clocked 1.5 hours that we have had foreplay with no erection. There are two times when I stopped when after about 10 minutes I realized that he wasn't going to participate. Those were the times he would just lie on his back with arms at his side with eyes closed, in his, "come and get it if you want it," pose!

Doc caught his contradictions. He said, "So you need her to initiate and then stimulate, but you feel under pressure when she wants sex?" I think Dick realized his contradictions.

Dick also said he enjoys the process more, and I seem to want just the end product/destination! I said I like and want both, not either. He said, "Well I didn't know sex was going to be so important to you!" WOW! WOW!!

Doc asked what he is doing to improve his sex life. His response was - eating better; eating foods that increase blood flow. Again, a contradiction: he is saying he doesn't have ED, and it is just that he needs stimulation; yet he is admitting to a need for increased circulation, which is an ED issue!

The "biggy" was when the doc asked him does he love me. He said "Yes." Then the doc asked does he want to be married to me. Dick said, "Uh... Ye...ah" in a tone like he was wondering if this is really true or not, but he thought it was what he should say! It was so unconvincing that the doc had a shocked look on his face! Yeah, I had that same look! Dick really doesn't want to be married to me! This is at the root of our issues then. This explains it all!

On another note, he talked about the fact that he'd had a past relationship where the woman controlled him to the point where he wasn't himself anymore, and thus he is very resistant to changing for anyone. The doc asked, "Even good change?" He said, "Well, yeah; good change." I noticed that he didn't state whether this was his first or second wife, but he has stated to me before that his first wife sought to control him.

He also said we don't have a lot of interests in common. This surprised me, because when we were dating, we had everything in common! He said when we were dating, he did things with me because he wasn't doing his thing anymore due to unemployment. He said he wants to do his old routine now, which is to go work out with his friends. I'm not stopping him! He's never once made plans to get with these friends, of whom I'm unaware. He said the local gym is just filling in the time until he does this.

He said when he gets home, he just wants to chill and he turns on MSNBC, but this doesn't do it for him. I don't know what he's getting at; he can do or watch whatever he wants. I leave him to himself, as he's told me he wishes. He stated that sitting on the couch with me is uncomfortable, which is why he sits on the floor or the other couch. I responded that he seemed to enjoy sitting close together watching TV when we dated. He said, "Yeah, and I was in pain doing it!" He clarified, saying that the couch made his back hurt. He's never indicated that he was in pain before.

He also said he thinks our age difference is an issue in our relating. He said I treat him like I'm his mom!!!!!! Ludicrous!!!!!!! While my mouth was hanging open, I was trying to think of what he's talking about. He has never, ever told me this before! So here are the things that I can think of that might be what he's referring to.

Before we married, he told me that I remind him of his mom, yet he quickly said, "And that's a good thing!" We had a good laugh that time I had a repair guy over, who used the bathroom without washing his hands and then touched the kitchen counter and other things. When he left, Dick and I went to every spot we recalled him touching, cleaning it with antibacterial cleaner! We laughed about it, and he told me this is just what his mom would do! There were other instances like that of which he's said I reminded him of his mom. But this is not treating him like I'm his mom; this is reminding him of his mom!

Another time, many months ago, I had asked him about why he was acting reserved, and he finally shared that it felt like I was controlling him. I needed an explanation, so he told me that sometimes I ask him to do things after work. The only things I could think of were asking him to either sweep the pool or wash the car. He confirmed this, and so I shared that the only reason I'd ask for this to be done on a weeknight was that it had been neglected weekends. Weekends, he should take care of these weekly tasks, but he doesn't. He knows that the pool gets green if not attended to, yet week after week he will not brush; he prefers to just skim the leaves off the top. I keep telling him that it is more important to sweep than to skim. The skimmer takes care of the skimming, but sweeping is a manual task that must be done at least once a week. Weekends he lies around watching TV all day, and there have been times on weekends I'd remind him about the pool, yet he'd respond like he was irritated that I said it. He'd say he was going to get to that. I know that sometimes he will go out there at night and turn on the pool light and sweep; he'll even clean the filter in the dark due to neglecting it in the day! So I learned not to say anything those weekends, assuming he was going to get to it later. Later, he'd be asleep on the couch though! I'd see the pool walls getting greener and greener; and I know when this is happens, the pool won't wait until another weekend! It will be all green by then. I choose not wake him up when he falls asleep in front of the TV on weekends. But I have to say something before the next weekend which therefore means it falls on a weeknight, when he still wants to chill.

The same holds true for the car. I used to have an unlimited monthly car wash membership, so my car was spotless every day. I had a reputation for such a spotless car back then. When we dated, he said I didn't have to pay for this service anymore; he'd take care of washing my car for me. So I quit the service, and he washed it almost weekly. Once married, it stretched out much longer. I waited for the times now and then that he'd wash it, because I didn't want to seem ungrateful in insisting on weekly washes from him. But my car was FILTHY! There is no reason that getting married should mean that I have to drive around in a filthy car! But this has been my reality for nine months now! I don't complain, but now and then, I have had to point out how my car is past due for a wash, and he finally washes it. Sometimes, this may fall on a weeknight. There's an easy solution to this problem: just do these tasks every weekend!

The other controlling thing that he had brought up in the past was that I expect him to come and eat dinner when he first gets home. He feels this is controlling behavior! WOW!!!!! I couldn't believe my ears! I was doing something that anyone else in the world would appreciate, but he sees it as controlling! I have dinner ready for him every night that he gets home from work. In fact, I work hard to time it so that it is hot and ready by 6 pm. I thought this was a great labor of love I gave him – a hot meal when he gets home from work. Instead, unbeknownst to me, he saw it as controlling. He said he wants to eat when he wants to eat. He may want to just kick back a while or go to the gym and then eat. I was accommodating. I said, "No problem. I'll just have it ready later then." He then said that if I'm hungry, to just go on and eat, and he'll eat when he feels like it. I asked, "Oh, then we'll be eating separately from now on?" He said "Yes." I said I didn't want to start a habit of eating apart. The dinner table is the only time when we come together weeknights. He realized this, so he conceded to us eating together, but on his timing. So we agreed that I'd have dinner ready after his workout. Since he doesn't work out daily, I asked him to call me from work those days he wasn't planning to work out, and I'd have dinner ready sooner. He neglected calling me those days, so for a while, I didn't have dinner ready when he got home and wanted to eat. So he changed it back to eating first, then going to the gym. Then it was back and forth again; so now, there's no real pattern.

It is just so peculiar to me that he saw this as controlling. I was accommodating, not controlling. I made sure whatever I was doing for the day stopped at a certain point in the afternoon so that my man had a hot meal when he arrived. But anyway, back to his mom, maybe it reminds him of having to wash his hands and eat at a certain time when growing up; my having a dinnertime was reminiscent of her. And in general, I believe that this points to that struggle he has with parental dependence and his projection of it to me through resistance! All I can say is... wow!!!

There is nothing else that he has pointed out, or that I've done that could be construed as mothering, except perhaps reminding/asking him to do things that were well overdue. I've asked/reminded him to make a doctor appointment with a specialist and to make an appointment with child support services to see about reducing this $77k bill that really isn't valid! These things are six months overdue, so of course I *bring them up! In fact, it was last month that I finally worked up the nerves to use the words, "I insist," in my request. This was when he jumped all over me, saying "Who do you think I am? Of course I know how to make an appointment... I'm a man! I won't have you treating me this way!"*

I can now translate that! He is saying, "Who do you think I am; your son? I'm a <u>grown</u> man, not your son, and I don't need my mom telling me what to do and how to do it!" Now it all makes sense! He is projecting his mom onto me!

A wife has a right to bring up issues that are overdue which affect the health of either party, the finances or the marriage. It is not mothering; it is partnering... looking out for my partner and our partnership. But since he is so delinquent in his responsibilities, he hears it more and more, and it reminds him of a mother.

*And to bring up the age difference is just a low blow!!!! [Pointing out that I am 5.5 years older than he.] He knows it has nothing to do with age, but he throws that out there, because the only fact in anything he said was that there is an age difference! So he said it to lend credence to his other false statements! Wow!*

*We were getting nowhere, and we were running out of time. I went ahead and read the first half of my "Journal Conclusion" to him. [Inserted here.]*

## JOURNAL CONCLUSION

At this point, I'm all fed up, I'm spent, I have nothing left, and something's gotta give! I can't take it anymore. This has been how I've been feeling for weeks now, and his display of attention and affection Sunday is just too late! It does not sway me! He has just run out of time!

Our relationship has flat-lined, and his use of paddles this weekend and this morning does not revive it! It is a sad reality, but so was my existence these last nine months of my life. It is inconceivable that I have been in a celibate marriage for nine months! It is a sad and sorry state of affairs that I found myself in, yet out of love and devotion, I stayed. But I stayed <u>assuming</u> that he would do his part also! I assumed that, surely, he wanted to change his condition and that as soon as we got coverage, he'd head to a specialist and continue under a doctor's care until there was improvement. I didn't think this was too far of a stretch of my imagination... to the point of assumption. But now I see that it must have been just my assumption, not his reality! Reality is – next week – he'll finally be seen by a specialist for his levels, which I believe to be at the root of his ED! [It turned out to be July!] I NEVER would have thought that he'd wait nine months into our marriage before getting a diagnosis and medical intervention from a specialist!

Well, who knows how long it takes for a woman to wait to see proactive progress in such a case; but apparently it is under nine months! I am so through! I'm done! I can't go on like this a week longer! And the fact that these last few days have been ideal doesn't change things. I am still resolute that there needs to be a major change in our status! Too late is too late! There wasn't a time period that I said I'd hang in there for resolution. That's not what I mean by "out of time!" I mean, that somehow, over the course of time, the lack of an intimate relationship coupled with the withholding of an affectionate connection caused the death of our marriage. I truly believe that were it not for the withholding of displays of affection and the extreme delay in my husband seeking treatment, I would not have run out of time already; the marriage would still have life. But I felt it dying on many occasions – each time that he stopped our connection and was aloof and unloving. And on a few of those occasions, I shared with him how I felt, only to be further mistreated with his defensive tone of voice, elevated voice, wagging head and jerky comments.

In retrospect, I realized that I was asking him to throw out a lifeline! I was saying, "Give me a reason to stay!" He always did the opposite! He pushed me away repeatedly by withholding attention and affection – our connection. Then to top it off, he never did take seriously the big job he had in front of him. He was to immediately get under a doctor's care for his presumed sugar problem, which was for his overall health and ultimately for the health of our sex life, thus, our marriage!

I've finally come to the point where I realize, "It is what it is!" That's a point of revelation and introspection. That's about when I started journaling (in May), and I asked myself the question, "Now can I deal with what it is?" The answer turned out to be "NO!" I am not coping well at all! I needed and sought out my therapist and continued with my introspection. After the revelation is the action step [the resolution]. See, there's actually a sense of relief, because when you realize "It is what it is," you can stop the exhaustive "hoping" to no avail! Before, you feel that the circumstances are controlling you and your feelings, but once you have the revelation, you realize that you can and should remove yourself from, or change the circumstances! Hence, the relief!

I struggled with this resolution for weeks; in fact, I delayed in journaling it, because once I wrote it, it would become real, and I'd act on it. Yes, change needs to happen, but it could be uncomfortable. But that's less important; change must happen, and it must happen now.

It was late May, when Dick was relaxing on one couch, and I on the other in the family room, that I realized that we were two separate souls co-existing. I looked over at him and asked myself, "Why is he here? What does he want? He obviously doesn't want me, so what does he want?" Did he just want a nice place to stay; someone with whom to share expenses – a roommate? Did he just have a desire to feel settled? We need to call it what it is then and stop stringing me along thinking we have a marriage! Well, it is a roommate situation, and I didn't sign up for that! Nor did I sign up for a marriage without sex!

So it's time to make a change! What has happened in our marriage is not okay, and we must make the necessary adjustments. Our relationship has flat-lined, and the only way to bring back the pulse is to have a separation with a purpose.

Dick might think that we can revive the pulse with attention to romance, but at this point that is a Band-Aid. It is the Band-Aid I've been pleading for over the course of our marriage, but it is the Band-Aid that he withheld, until surgery is the only option left. Those Band-Aids I was asking for before would have perhaps stopped the bleeding while we dealt with the actual injury; but I'm all bled out now, and the injury is too grave. I cannot continue without some major reconstructive changes. I've been walking around these past few weeks saying, "I can't take it anymore; I can't live like this; I won't live like this!"

We've got to start all over if our marriage is to survive. We need to live apart while going to counseling to work through our issues. Our issues aren't just sexual and financial, nor are they just the lack of connection. It is the way we can't resolve any of these issues, because his response when I bring them up is worse than the issues themselves! These responses show me that I am not in his heart. I'm in his life, I'm on his marriage certificate, but I'm not in his heart.

In essence, I'm saying he does not really love me as a wife. And he certainly is not "in love with me." For months and months, every night in bed I used to tell him that I love him, and he'd reply with the same. It bothered me that he never initiated it, and I wasn't even convinced when he'd echo it. I finally asked him about it and told him I'd really like to hear it first, and regularly, but he just blew that request off. A person will tell you who they are and how they feel about you. You just have to listen. I did. He isn't telling me because he doesn't. A few months ago, I decided to stop telling him, so now, it is never spoken.

Last month when I asked him if he was "in love with me," he answered "Yes," and when I asked how he knew, his first response was, "Because I know that I don't want to lose you." Then he followed up with responses very generic to anyone; not a wife. Well, he must have been aware that his behavior could lead to losing me, and he was right. But he's only losing me partially. We will not be cohabitating any longer, but we will be man and wife seeking to re-establish a marital bond. And if Dick is interested in this re-establishment, then lucky for him – it is all within his power. Through our counseling sessions, we'll pour through the issues and make resolutions that will become the building blocks of a healthy marriage.

*He didn't seem surprised. In fact, he said he couldn't say that much of what I said wasn't true! He said he disagreed with some things, but that it was mostly true. Doc clarified what a "separation with a purpose" is and asked him if he was in agreement with the separation conclusion. He nodded and said that might be what we need.*

*Then he went on some tangents, so I brought him back to the separation by reading the last half of my nine page doc. [Inserted here.]*

Here is another factor in my assessment of the state of our marital affairs and my resultant separation resolution. "I feel defrauded!" I felt like this since September 19$^{th}$, 2013! This was when, on my wedding night, I discovered that my husband is <u>impotent</u>! After a long period of foreplay, I noticed that my new husband's penis never arose. In fact, I remember thinking that it seemed as though he were just going through the motions of giving extensive foreplay; it seemed devoid of passion. It just seemed like he was "doing his job", systematically going from mouth to breasts on down, but not really that into me. Then, he rolled over and held me and went to sleep! I was dumbfounded, confused, disappointed, hurt, etc.! It turns out, to him, "foreplay" doesn't mean "before" intercourse; it means "instead" of intercourse! I don't think I slept a wink that night! I decided to give him the benefit of the doubt and attribute it to being fatigued.

The next morning we tried again to no avail. And again, that night! At some point, I decided to ask him if he had something he needed to share with me. He said "No." I brought up the fact that there have been no erections. He blamed it on several things. Me mostly! He said that he needs more stimulation. He also said that for a whole year, I've insisted on a celibate courtship, so how can I expect it to just rise now! [Actually, we had both agreed on dating without sex, based on our biblical beliefs.] I cried, because I just couldn't believe that "doing it God's way" could result in this. But I really didn't believe his excuse, so I pressed on, asking when he first noticed the ED. He tried to claim he didn't have ED, but admitted there were prior times that he didn't have erections. But he also claimed that during our engagement, he'd wake up at home with erections! I didn't want him to feel badly, so I didn't press the issue.

But night after night, after he'd gone to sleep, I'd sit in a bath of hot water in that big tub next to the bed [at a beautiful beach resort] and ponder the circumstance I'd walked into – and it kept pointing to the fact that Dick had <u>defrauded</u> me! He knew that he had a problem with erections, yet he did not tell me! In fact, he used to talk about how we were going to have to make up for lost time; how he'd come home stripping off his clothes and "do me" right on the kitchen counter; and how we'd have to get window coverings for the family room, because we'd be "doing it" in there all the time! He made me think we'd be very sexually active! He knew better, but he failed to disclose this critical piece of information!

He defrauded me, and this was the basis of the start of our marriage! Each night in that tub, I'd reflect on this and wondered if I should annul the marriage. Yet, out of love and devotion, I stayed. But as I said, I stayed based on him seriously addressing the issue. As soon as we got covered, I researched medical plans and got us signed up by end of November. I also researched doctors and made a recommendation of a primary care physician with an endocrine specialty and asked him to make an appointment for early December. But he refused to go with my recommendation and stretched out the timeline of being treated by an endocrinologist until... next week. [It turned out to be July! That's seven and a half months after he was eligible!] Over that period, every time I asked him to see a specialist, he argued and didn't. But what he didn't realize is that, each time he didn't, and with every week and month that passed, I realized that treating his ED wasn't that important to him, and hence, our sex life. And hence our intimacy and marriage weren't that important to him. Our relationship as I knew it died in this interim, and so did any hope of a fulfilling one in the future.

So, I was defrauded from the beginning, and he continued to defraud me of any medical resolution of this ED situation. Fraud is a major issue; fraud is grounds for the forfeiture of any contractual agreement. I went far beyond any reasonable attempt to continue, in light of this! I am not calling for the voiding of the marriage contract though, but for the reconstruction of the contract right now – through separation.

But this isn't the only area in which I was defrauded. I was defrauded out of money. At the time, I believed that there was absence of malice; that Dick did not intentionally defraud me out of money. But the end result is the same. Thousands of my pre-marriage dollars were spent on marriage related items, when in fact, he was to have repaid me once married, but didn't. This arrangement was due to the fact that his permanent position and raise hadn't been granted yet. [But later I realized that there was malice; he had deceived me about his availability of funds.]

So, the only money available to spend on our plans came from me. [But in hindsight, I see that the fraud started even before the engagement.] One time when we were waiting on a movie (long before it was even time to ring shop), we strolled into a jeweler and tried on rings. He had me try on a ring that was soooooo out of his price range. I thought we were just messing around, but he insisted that this is just the type of ring he wanted to buy me. Dick started then and continued telling me he wanted to get me a ring that would, "make my friends jealous!" So when it was time to ring shop, the extra wide band was what we shopped for. We found this ring eventually, which was priced less than half the prices we were seeing elsewhere!

According to our initial timeline of getting engaged with enough time to plan a small wedding prior to Jane going away to college, we needed to go ahead with the ring purchase. Yet Dick was still awaiting his raise, so we agreed that I'd purchase it and he'd repay me. So when it was time to purchase my engagement ring, I fronted the money. [Stupid!]

Now, when I wear it, people gawk at it and say things like, "Wow, your husband really loves you!" And the most frequent comment is, "Wow, what does your husband do for a living?" I have no response because my husband didn't buy it! And also, when we're together and get comments, Dick gives this cocky response and takes credit for buying it for me! This really, really hurts, because he knows he didn't! He knows that I bought it, and he never said a word about it to me! I feel defrauded! Every day when I put this ring on, I think about how he was happy to use my pre-marriage dollars to say that he got me this ring; and it stings.

But there was another instance where thousands of my pre-marriage money was spent on our behalf, before we wed, and it went for naught. I put down $3k on an African safari trip we were supposed to have taken in February 2014, because again, Dick's money had not come through on the job yet. My issue is not that I paid the deposit; if he had paid the balance as we had agreed, and had gone, it would have been all good. But we didn't go, and I lost my deposit because he couldn't get his passport due to past due child support! While he didn't do this on purpose, his negligence resulted in my forfeiture of $3k (not to mention the forfeiture of the costly airline tickets charged to my card once married!!)!!! Dick's negligence was in not reporting to CSS, January 2012 that he was unemployed with no income at all. They would have adjusted his child support figure accordingly. But he failed to do this at any point in his unemployment. Before we married, I point blank asked him if he was going to be responsible for paying back child support for the year and a half that he was unemployed and didn't pay. He point blank answered, "No!" We got married and they garnished his wages for arrears, which precludes him from passport qualification! He has always retorted to me, any time that I bring up correcting the issue, that he's been in the system for 20 years and I haven't, so he knows what to do; I don't! Yet, with 20 years of experience, he failed to do the very thing that would have kept us from owing $11k of arrears!!!!!!!!!!!!!!

It is bad enough, that $11k is exiting our budget for something he technically doesn't owe; but resultantly, I lost $3k, and he hasn't so much as apologized for it!!!!! This tore a huge gouge in me emotionally because I felt so taken advantage of by him. More than getting the money back, I wanted Dick to "man-up" and come to me and say, "Baby, I know that my inaction caused you to lose your $3k trip deposit last year, and I am so sorry. I want to make it up to you because that was your money that you made before we were even married. I'm going to pay you back in installments." This was actually a fantasy. Again, not only because I'd be reimbursed, but because it would be Dick owning his complicity in his own child support matter which affected my finances. I wanted him to come correct and take responsibility. I wanted to feel that I wasn't defrauded in yet another way.

So, these two pre-marital financial losses have compounded the "other" defrauding, and I just feel "ass-out!" I feel exposed, and the one exposing me is my own husband! I really feel that if he had wanted to "cover me" as a husband is supposed to do, when he finally did get his pay increase he should have come to me and said: "Now it's time for me to repay you, because you paid for my obligations when we were dating, and it put you out of THOUSANDS of dollars. Here's a start dear, and there's more to come each month!" This shouldn't be just my fantasy; if he were a real husband, he would do this! Even someone who is not a spouse – who made a person forfeit their money – should make amends!

This is just a deep wound that has been wide open for nine months, and only Dick can close it. I need Dick to close this wound in me, so that we as a couple can heal!

*Dick argued with me about the trip deposit, saying he never wanted to go anyway! I said that he never told me this; just before the deposit was due, I asked him if we were doing this, and he said, "Yes." He didn't have the money; he had just gotten his job, but we agreed that I was making the deposit, and he'd pay the balance which was due in eight months. I reiterated that I never would have paid on something that he said he didn't want to do. He admitted that he never said no, but doesn't remember saying yes. I said it would have been asinine for me to have proceeded with paying out $3k if he never said yes to the trip! This was a smokescreen, and I kept bringing him back to what I had read; that if he had paid the balance due and we had gone, it would have been a non-issue. But the fact that we couldn't go, and I lost the deposit due to his fault was unacceptable; he needed to take responsibility for that! He finally said, "Do you want me to pay you back?" I answered, "Yes!" He said, "Fine!", that he would.*

*He said, "So, this was all about money?" I responded, "No, this is a ten-page document, and the money was talked about only on the last few pages!" He asked, "Then what happened to the $11k I gave you?" I'm like, "What?" He said, "Yeah, I've paid you over $11k since we've been married! I know you don't have $11k worth of utility bills!" I said, "But I have a mortgage!" He said, "Well my name is not on the mortgage, so I shouldn't have to cover any of that!" Wow! Wow!!!*

Both the doc and I had that same shocked look! Wow! What did he just say? Wow!

He believes that he can live here rent/mortgage free! Wow! I just can't get past... "Wow!" Yes, he said this is what he believes! He continued, "Well, you paid your mortgage without me before we were married. Why should I have to pay on it now?" Wow!!!!!! This is it! This is "critical mass"! This is the point that all our financial issues hinge on. This is why I've had so much of a problem getting him to cover half our living expenses. Because he really believes that he shouldn't have to!!!!! It is unfathomable!!!! Where does he think he can live rent free? Why does he think he should live rent free, just because his name is not on the mortgage? [Lord, Jesus, I'm so glad that I didn't put his name on my mortgage!!! This house is for my kids to inherit, not for an ex-spouse!] Why does he think he gets to live in this house without contributing to the house note, and - have his kids live here part-time too? How can anyone even think this way??? This is why he'd ask for just the electric bill and cable bill. He figures that's all he and his kids use!!!! Unbelievable!!!!!!!!!!!

We had run out of time by this point, and the doc said, regardless as to whose name is on a note, two adults sharing a house should share that expense. As we were leaving, Dick asked if he could meet with him alone, and the doc replied to just make an appointment. I had gotten us a $2^{nd}$ evening appointment for July $14^{th}$, and we will both seek follow-up appointments, together and alone.

## Chapter 8: THE RESET BUTTON IS PUSHED!

July 1st, 2014

A week and a day after our 1st meeting with the therapist, I got a call from his office that an appointment became available tomorrow at 5:15. Dick says he can make it. Our week has been peaceful. Maybe that's because we haven't talked money or about the things he hasn't taken responsibility for. I haven't had to bring up bills yet, but today I will have to, since they're due in two days. When he told me he canceled his doctor appointment again, I didn't respond. If his health and the health of our marriage are that unimportant to him, this proves that our separation is necessary. He canceled his Thursday appt. because his eldest son needed to finish his FAFSA, and Dick's tax return had not been filed, so he chose to go to the IRS office instead of the doctor's office. He wasn't even going to tell me this, but I had asked him the night before about the time we should depart the next morning for his doc appt., so he told me he'd canceled it. I then asked him when his CSS appointment was, and he said he still hadn't reached them... telephone tag for a month he claims!

Dick has been more attentive and has actually initiated "sex attempts" several times this week. I'm sure that it's because of the impending separation. Saturday night, Sunday morning and Monday night, he initiated. This is a first! He's never, in over nine months of marriage, attempted sex even three times in a month, much less, three times in a week, on consecutive days!!! Last night, with a lot of stimulation, his *penis extended a little. It never got hard though. Yet he didn't try to use it, and it shrank back.*

He has shown a definite pattern of dishing it out and actually having slight penile response, only when there is an impending change in our status. He actually uses the lack of sex to control me and the futile attempts at sex to reel me back in! Whoa!!! This is sick!

## SEPARATION PLANS

*Saturday, we had a very leisurely day; I did some housework, and he did yard work. We swam, and afterwards when we were chilling in the family room, I said that we should address the elephant in the room. He looked around for it as a joke and then went right back to what he was reading. I waited and said it again. He indicated to go on, and I said we should talk about our imminent change in living arrangements. He said he had looked at places and he was planning on moving the next week. He said we could try a six-month separation, and if ready under six months, that's fine. He said that we can have Rev. class and Sundays after church as date times. We'd sit together as normal and not have to share our separation status with others. He said he'd take his couch and table and bookcase, and he'd probably leave the bed. This morning he had checked out one place.*

# DUPLICITOUS

### July 2nd, 2014

He didn't come to our 2nd counseling session, allegedly due to a meeting at work starting and ending late... so he says. However, when he finally called to say that he was too far away to make it, I noticed that the ambient sounds gave him away; he wasn't in a moving car! I asked him where on the freeway he was, and he was very vague. This is because he really was at home and lied about being on the road. Also confirming my suspicion is that I left the doc's office then, and when I got home ten minutes later, he was already there. Dick could not have made it home and changed his clothes that quickly from where he vaguely said he was on the freeway. He just wasn't planning on another counseling session.

### July 3rd, 2014

Today, bill payment day, Dick sneaked out this morning without kissing me and without leaving a check on the night stand. The nerve of him! He generated these bills with me since April, but didn't pay them!

Last night he had promised a good foot rub, as if this were supposed to placate me! A foot rub, in exchange for paying bills... no thanks! It wasn't even one of his good ones! While getting my feet rubbed, I reminded him of the outstanding bills and the due date the next day, and he said "Ok." I also asked about his apartment hunt, and he said one was pricy, and he's going to look at another.

Today, I told my sister, and she was so surprised and hurt for me. I told her not to be. I told her if she had known, the time to hurt was when I was going through it with him. But now, I've extracted myself from the neglect of this husband of mine! I am now fine! I'm back! Yea!

Tonight when I got home, he was in the driveway, and he said to roll up the windows and he'd wash my car. This was a nice buffer; I was very grateful. At dinner, I told him I was unhappy that he didn't leave a check for his half of bill payment. He said it was because he'd found a place that he's moving into on Sunday, and that he doesn't know what he'll owe until his credit is run and he signs the agreement on Sunday. He said he'll know what he can pay on Monday.

July 4th, 2014

His kids went with their mom out of town, so this was a great surprise weekend for us. He hadn't told me nor planned anything for us.

MY INDEPENDENCE DAY!

July 6th, 2014

It is Sunday afternoon, and Dick is now moving into his new apartment. He went straight from church and signed the lease and moved in. I went mattress shopping. When I returned, he had emptied half his clothes from the closet and was out.

We've related so well this past week; it reminded me of pre-marriage days. He is so happy about leaving that he has a real good attitude. He's showing much attention and affection. Wow, if only he had kept this up during the marriage! [This is good, but puzzling. If he's so glad to get away from me, why is he now affectionate towards me? And if he wants to be affectionate towards me, then why is he so glad to get away from me? It all goes back to control of sex and finances! He wasn't planning on contributing either!]

We watched "Black Nativity", "Robocop" and "Iron Man II" together and enjoyed it. He went to bed with me and stayed in bed the mornings of Independence Day, Saturday and Sunday! [It may seem funny to state that he went to bed with me, but in this sick marriage, he did everything he could – not to go to bed when I did, and to be out of bed when I woke up.] He hasn't attempted sex lately, but he hugs, holds and kisses me, in and out of bed. He had made breakfast for me Saturday; something he hasn't done in a minute! He voluntarily washed my car last Thursday and cleaned the grill before and after we BBQ'd on Friday. He was attentive before and after church. He even kissed me when he put me in my car. He is really trying, and I appreciate that!

[This is an edit from March 4$^{th}$, 2015: In re-reading this, I realize that all this nice behavior is again, his control of me. It is his dishing out what he knows he's been withholding, due to the imminent change in our status. It is also because he wasn't planning on paying me back, but had to act nice to keep me in the dark about it until he could get his stuff out! I wasn't going to do a "Waiting to Exhale" burn scene! But being the eternal optimist that I am, back then I labeled it as, "really trying, and I appreciate that!" Wow, Janice, when are you going to learn? He still had me fooled!]

*The two weekends in a row without the kids meant that he didn't wear the "daddy only" hat; it really made things feel more like a marriage should. We didn't have the roller coaster effect of him going offline as a husband for days and then taking more days to recover. We've had continuous relating, and it's been real good. Plus, he's trying real hard, since we're on the blink (and perhaps since he's happy to leave).*

This is how it should have been all along! We could have made it if it had been! The problem hadn't been the presence of his kids every other weekend; it was that he never knew how to keep his "husband hat" on once his "daddy hat" went on. Thus, the loss of momentum caused the loss of real relating... not to mention the absence of a sex-life.

# PHASE 3 – BACK ON TRACK!

## Chapter 9: MY JOURNEY BEGINNING – NO LONGER DERAILED!

*Sunday, September 14th, 2014*

*It has been about two months since I've journaled. I know that this is due to the fact that I've been enjoying my sense of relief since my new-found freedom. I didn't want to revisit something that was so close to the pain that I was experiencing when I was in the midst. Though journaling was great therapy for me, it was still tied to the pain that I was in, so I took a break from it. Plus, it was not as necessary, since I had changed the circumstances I was in.*

Wow, it is great to hear me say that! <u>I'm used to just suffering under the burden, because I mistakenly used to think that those were the cards dealt to me. I now know that I was wrong.</u> Isn't that something we Christians do? We think God has us in the circumstance, so we work on aligning our attitudes with gratitude, thinking we're doing something Christlike! But as we journey through life, there will be adverse experiences; even those that we choose, thinking that it was God's will. Sometimes our choices are wrong. So when we encounter such circumstances, we must not let them derail us for long on our journey. We must get back on our path as quickly as possible.

<u>I shall get on with my life! I shall live!!! I will not stay derailed! I will get back on the right path. I realize now that I was on the wrong path for a long time, which is how I ended up so far off path! So actually, I've been derailed since before I married the wrong man, which is why I married the wrong man! But this failed 10 month marriage is what woke me up and got me back on the right path! So, I finally found the silver lining – I'm no longer derailed.</u>

*When I was saving the short entry above just now, I was saving it at the end of my "Journal Conclusion" doc [document] from before, thinking that I was just adding a few more insights. Yet, it occurred to me that it should be a new doc, and I should give it a new title: "Journey Beginning!" Yes, I took the steps to recognize my marital derailing and changed my situation, and here I am on the other side. But since I now recognize that my derailing started before the marriage, I must continue journaling to find out why. So actually, my journey has just begun! And as God would have it, today, 1st Lady [now she is Pastor Renee!] spoke about "our journey," teaching that we should continue it, even when we find ourselves "in the midst." She gave dozens of synonyms and their definitions. I jotted down the ones that I connected with: expedition, excursion, odyssey, safari, survey, and sojourn. The antonyms I related to were derail and detour.*

I've been derailed, and I have to get back on track. Just getting rid of the unhealthy marriage isn't enough. I still have to now jump back on that track! <u>That wrong track was that of living life too small, too cautiously and too contently, which is what made me willing to settle for the type of man I married. My derailment's first name was "caution", its middle name was "contentment", and its last name was "complacency"!</u> I have a big life to live out in this great big world that my God made! I am not honoring Him by playing it safe; staying put; being quiet; being content living on just an early retirement income; being happy with just this plot of land; living within a small set income and keeping my expenses down; being happy to get senior discounts; enjoying a lower bill because I'm sweating out the sweltering summer; driving a car without A/C, and sometimes without power steering and a horn; and being committed (rather, trapped) to a man who gave me NOTHING in return.

## BE GRATEFUL, BUT NOT CONTENT OR COMPLACENT!

*Sometimes, I let things go on for too long, because I'm always trying to find the good in it. I'm just so positive, that I try to convert all my negatives into positives. I try to be content, which resulted in complacency. But some things I just must let go of! And sometimes I must actively seek change! In fact, Oprah did a "Life Class" on Robin Roberts the other day; her insights were so profound that I found myself taking notes. She said that "We should be grateful, but never content!"*

I understand and agree with that now. But I had made them interchangeable in my life; being content with the status-quo has been an underlying theme of my life. My gratitude led me to be content with what I have, because God gave it to me. But this has really kept me bound and not allowed me to reach my full potential. That's really something, because to me they were synonyms; because I am innately a truly grateful person, I let myself live in a rut called "contentment", which led to complacency! Wow! Well, no more!

[As I stated in the Preface, I was vulnerable for a reason. I have to take some responsibility for falling prey. My complicity was in my complacency. Thus, I had to make a Revision Decision about it as well...]

I will Live Life Loud! Riding "The Beast" this past May in Puerto Rico was part of that resolve! It is the biggest, baddest zip line in the world! I will take and <u>make</u> adventures for myself! I will stretch myself outside of my comfort zone. I will set and achieve goals, some of which are to create businesses out of the witty ideas that God has given me. I also want to teach the Book of Revelation in my church. And my fun goal is to take my Chicago Steppin' to the next level! [About a year after this comment, I began to teach the Book of Revelation for my church, Point of Grace (POG)!]

## "GOALMATE... NOT SOULMATE!"

On the relational front, I will no longer date complacent men. And at this stage of life, if they're complacent, they're probably "losers". And typically, men who are "losers" are "users"! I will date grown men; men who are going places in life and have their own! I won't even limit myself to men who are not "geographically desirable"!

I am single! I am fine! I have kids who are grown and on their own! I am retired! I am not tied to a job! I am an innovator! Yet, I was willing to be tied down to a man who had all the opposites! What's <u>love got to do with it? Yeah, I loved him, but he zapped the very life out of me in just ten months! Actually, less! Why should I turn my very life over to him? That's not loving me or honoring God.</u>

*I'm now looking for a "goalmate", not a "soulmate". Big difference... big life lesson! All these years, I've been looking for my soulmate, and by its definition, I seemed to have found those qualities in Dick. We definitely had connected intensely on so many levels. But we had none of the same goals, and that made life miserable with him (but the fraud was the major culprit). Yeah, and one basic goal of mine was to have a sex life; boy... that wasn't one of his goals! I'm always reminded of his retort at our counseling session, "Well, I didn't know sex was going to be so important to you!" Yeah... not on the same page!*

*Since I've stated that my personal goal is to LIVE LIFE LOUD, I can't do that cooped up in the house with a man glued to the TV! I need to be out and about! That of course means travel too (and Dick couldn't even get a passport!)! I've gotta see this wonderful world that God has created, and I'd like to do this with my partner!*

My goalmate doesn't have to have all these goals, but he at least must not be an obstacle to any of them. <u>I coined the term "goalmate" to suggest that a couple needs not only to be on the same page in terms of goals, but in the same stage in life so that together they are ready to step into the next chapter in life!</u> Growing and creating that exciting next chapter is my goal; not just living in a holding pattern!

And unlike the supposition that there is only one "soulmate" out there for you (and I take exception to this notion), there can be many, many goalmates out there, with whom you can have a great relationship. To me, in my current stage of life, it is more practical to have a goalmate; yet in my younger stages, I desired my soulmate.

## ADJUST YOUR GOALS FOR GROWTH!

*Back to what I learned from Robin Roberts: She so embraced not being content, that when she was offered her dream job – the one she had set her sights on for years – she turned it down for a small-time job that would make her grow, so that she'd be better at her dream job when it rolled around again! Great move! And when it did come back around again, she took it, but then quickly got a better job offer doing something very different that would again stretch her. She left her goal job for this job she had never even considered!*

It's okay to change your goals as long as they better serve your life. We might set our goals to accommodate our desired trajectory from "A" to "Z", but sometimes our goals just get us moving in the right direction, but to a different outcome, one piece at a time. So we might just get to point "B", then have to re-evaluate. God's the only omniscient one! We don't always know the best path; we don't know what's around the bend. Robin Roberts was able to quickly assess her changing needs, thus she changed her goals, or at least changed the timeline to accommodate her new-found realizations.

<u>Personally, I hadn't yet realized that my new-found interests and life goals meant that I should have adjusted what I was looking for in a mate.</u> So when Dick came along, since he matched my old stage of life to which I had been accustomed, he seemed ideal. But I realized later that I had a new chapter coming, and he was still living out the old chapter. That was his stage of life, and that is fine; we all move throughout the stages of life. But ideally we should be in the same stages so that we don't find ourselves on different pages.

But I would not have ended the marriage over such. We would have just had to work on it. It was the fraud that doomed our marriage from the start! But I shouldn't be so hard on myself for my choice. My desire all my life had been to be happily married. After my first divorce, I had wasted 15 years of my life pining away "in love with love" and never finding the embodiment of it! Then, I finally thought that I had found it embodied in this man... and he wanted to marry me! And so I did. But I had not realized that in those 15 years, maybe some of my ideals for a mate should have changed; especially as I entered into a new stage of life. My new ideal for a mate should have been a goalmate.

It just occurred to me, that this 15 year obsession with getting married had been my idol! I had an idol, and didn't know it. Just because I masked it with asking God to provide the object of the idolatry, doesn't mean that it wasn't an idol! "God, bless me with a husband!" My mantra of 15 years! Wow! I was an idol worshipper. Lord, please forgive me! I repent!

## Chapter 10:  DIVORCE DECISION

*Sunday, September 14th, 2014 (cont'd)*

I've done a lot of journaling today. This Sunday afternoon, I've just had an outpouring of revelation. I also became keenly aware that God has put a book in me... unbeknownst to me! I am to publish my revelation filled journal as a book! I'm letting that sink in! But since I've not journaled in two months, here is a little catch-up.

### REJECTION REFLECTION/FLASHBACK

In July, the agreement was for us to see each other at church and Rev. class, and to go on dates. We hadn't gotten around to the dates, but Dick came to church the Sunday he was scheduled to teach the kids; I gave him his mail when he walked me to my car. He came to Rev. class, and when he walked me to my car afterwards, he then went to his car and returned with a hanger of mine that he had taken. Like I was concerned about that or even knew about it!

This, in retrospect, is one of those kinds of things he does to make it seem like he is totally honest and looking out for me; but in reality, he isn't. Returning a hanger? Really? The other thing he did that falls into this category is to ask me if I wanted him to follow me home to take the trash cans back in! Like I'm gonna say "Yes," drive 12 miles roundtrip just to take my cans in! He knew I'd say "No thanks." And how ironic, because a few days later, when he had come over to get things of his from the garage, the cans were sitting right there in front of the door, but he kept walking around them instead of taking them in!

He is such a hypocrite. He does or says things that fall in line with being about the business, but he does not follow through or do the things that really show that he's genuine... <u>like paying me back the thousands of dollars he owes me!</u>

*Speaking of money: He had never made a July payment, so at the end of July, I had emailed him about the outstanding CC debt he had left me with, with an attached spreadsheet that I had been showing him since April. I asked him to send a payment in the mail for the August bill. He emailed back stating that all his money was tied up with his kids' back to school expenses, so he was unable at the time. Silly me; I took this to mean that next month he would!*

*Well, he did a disappearing act from that point until present! We were supposed to have continued seeing each other at church and at Rev. class. He only made an appearance at Rev. class on 8/25 to teach in Dr. Z.'s absence [at the teacher's request back in early July for us both to teach class]. He did not make eye contact with me nor speak to me. I handed him his mail as people were speaking to him after class, then I left.*

*In fact, I had met with Dr. Z. a week before that to tell him that I couldn't lead the class with Dick due to the state of affairs. He knew nothing of our separation, so I shared for three hours. He then asked me if I still loved Dick, and I answered "Yes"; I really felt that it was still true. Dr. Z. too said that he could tell that I did. Dr. Z. wanted to* speak with Dick too (being a marriage and family counselor), but Dick wouldn't respond to his text messages to talk; he only confirmed that he would teach that class in August.

He had also confirmed with me, although we had separated, his plans to attend our friends' August wedding. So I RSVP'd for us and went to Kim and Ed's wedding that month, totally expecting Dick to show, thinking that surely he wouldn't let them down. He did let them down! He not only didn't show, but I found out later that he had never even contacted them before the wedding to change his RSVP. Dick did the same thing regarding his obligation to teach kids' Sunday school once a month. Although in July he showed, in August, he didn't show, nor did he even inform the Sunday school department of his quitting! This is low!

Rev. class was dark for Labor Day, but the next week, I kept looking for him to come [stupid, huh?], even saving a seat for him. But he didn't. And the realization set in that at all costs, he was avoiding me, because by then, he was already four months late getting a repayment to me. I now realized that he was never intending on repaying me. I began to accept that I had been conned. And that's when I let my love go.

<u>It's one thing for him to have health problems initially beyond his control, and even to temporarily withhold my repayments due to his kids' expenses; but to con me – never intending on repaying me is inexcusable! It shows total malice and no regard for me, and no love for me. It was all a farce; so then, letting go was finally easy! I had been in love with a manufactured image; when I discovered the total fraud that he was, the love evaporated with the image. The good man that he projected himself to be was a vapor, and so my love vaporized with this realization. And no,</u>

it wasn't a case of, "good man – just bad husband." No; any husband who would defraud his wife is not a good man in any respect! He can be as gracious to people as he wants, quote scripture, and teach as many Rev. classes as he wants, but if he continues to defraud his wife, there is evil present.

So, I didn't lose any more time after that. I started working on my divorce filing. I did all my research and started my paperwork. I also made an appointment for that week to fill Pastor Ken in on our separation and my recent decision to divorce.

Until now, it took three hours to explain the farce of our marriage to people, but this time it only took 1.5 hours after I read my journal conclusion to Pastor Ken. He was surprised that we were even having marital troubles, and he said that normally he advises couples to stick with their marriages, but not in my case. He assessed from what I told him that Dick had abandoned me, and I needed to go on and divorce him.

When sharing with him about the sexual dysfunction and his resultant loss of interest in sex, I speculated that it seems to have led to a sexual crisis for him, where he is perhaps questioning the importance of sex and a wife in his life. His lack of sexual arousal and attraction to his wife doesn't mean that he is attracted to men, but it probably has him confused. So Pastor Ken helped me to better phrase it: Dick is perhaps "struggling with his sexual identity," trying to learn how he now relates to sex. Pastor Ken also confirmed another thing that I had already been thinking... which is that what I had written and had read to him was the beginning of a book!

September 16th, 2014

Dick surprisingly showed up to Rev. class last night. He actually went and sat at a different table from me, even though the only other seat at my table was empty. Then he tried to act like he was oblivious to anyone around him, keeping his head down and busying himself with his papers! It was utterly ridiculous! Then, the thought popped into my head that a classmate who always comes in late with her friend would ask me to give up my seat for them and sit with my husband. Sure enough, that's exactly what happened; so I was ready with my answer, "I was here already." She asked, "Then can he sit with you?" I said, "You can ask him." She had this confused look on her face, but asked him, and he complied. He said not a word to me. Ridiculous! Again, the thought popped into my head that he would run for the door after prayer, so be ready! And so I was! I had my bag and was ready to run, and I called out to him as he hit the door! So as not to make a scene, he turned around. I called him over to me, away from others who were near the door.

His countenance showed disdain for me; he showed no openness towards me or remorse for his behavior of the past months. But I continued. I said that we really ought to talk to Dr. Z. He said he had no time; he had to pick up his daughter. I said, "Not tonight. Are you available to talk tomorrow night?" He said that there was a lot coming up at work. I asked if any of it took place tomorrow night. He said, "No." I said "then let's see if Dr. Z. is available Tuesday night." He again insisted that he had to pick up his daughter. I said it will be just a second, and I quickly got the affirmative from Dr. Z. for Tuesday. Dick agreed and quickly left.

As an aside, Dr. Z. seems to think that Dick is just hurting, and will come around. I'm so surprised that he doesn't see the real picture. We were in greater harmony after the separation than in marriage. It was only when I asked him to continue to repay me that he cut me off completely, which revealed to me his complete fraudulent character! That has nothing to do with hurting, and everything to do with being willing to hurt another – his wife! And sure enough, this "hurting" husband quickly canceled our counseling session the next day! If he were hurting so much, he would have been glad to be counseled by someone he knows and loves, who happens to be a marriage and family therapist.

So, today after receiving his cancellation text, I resolved to get my divorce! No more chances! I gave him many chances during our marriage: I gave him a chance through counselling, and then through separation, and then through offering counselling through Dr. Z.; but he refused! So no more chances! Time's up! Our 1st anniversary is coming up Friday, and I resolve to file on that date!


September 30th, 2014

I need to keep listening to the Holy Spirit and quit looking at circumstances! Don't keep getting derailed! The Holy Spirit has already led me to the Revision Decision, but I kept giving Dick chances. Dick wasn't serious about meeting; he was saving face in front of Dr. Z. So, that Tuesday, 9/16, when Dick canceled our meeting, I canceled any more chances and proceeded with divorce! In fact, I got right on the phone and invited five special ladies to come over on my anniversary for dinner, drinks and conversation from the heart. That was when I confided in Kim, Sanya and Pam about our situation... from "A" to "Z"! They were all so shocked and hurt. I even broke out the 1-year-old slice of wedding cake from the freezer and ceremoniously washed it down the garbage disposal! [Mildred and the Rev. class had given us a wedding cake in class after we married.] I tried to get with Teresa and my cousins Ethel and Brenda that following Saturday to inform them, but they were unavailable.

<u>The other thing I did earlier that day on 9/19 was to file for divorce! What a way to celebrate my 1st wedding anniversary!</u> It was so convenient to be able to file electronically. There was no option for annulment, so I added it as an attachment, and for this reason, the next week I was told that it would have to be modified. So, the actual date on the filing is 9/25, and it wasn't accepted by the court until today, 9/30. I wanted him e-served, but that isn't offered to Family Law filers, so I'll have to have him served.

Today, while out on errands and before going to the gym, I got four calls of encouragement. Sharon, Kim and Janice called, and then Stanton called, and we talked (as I sat in front of the Upland Mountain Green strip mall, viewing the beautiful mountain landscape). As an attorney, he gave me the advice that I should go ahead and hire a professional server. So, I will research this on Wednesday. It would be great if I could actually have him served on Oct 1st. I will try.

October 1st, 2014

Today, I found a process server in Riverside who will be able to serve him the next day, and I can just email him the docs and pay online for just $55! This is such a relief. I didn't have to print out forms; I just emailed my files to the server. I'm so hyped! He'll be served tomorrow, and after I walk my proof of service in for filing, I can sit back for 30 days and wait for his response, and then go to court for our hearing next month!

October 3rd, 2014

Hallelujah!!!! At 9:19 am (wow, what an omen: 9/19 is our wedding date and the date I filed for divorce) I got a call from the server saying "I served him"! Great; I'm on my way!

## Chapter 11: FROM MY "EX" TO MY "NEXT"!

October 3rd, 2014 (cont'd)

And check this! I had Dick served today, and tomorrow I have a date with Stanton! You go girl!!!

[Oh, about Stanton: Stanton is the man I had dated just prior to dating and marrying Dick. I've known Stan since I was 14, but hadn't seen him since college. I had always looked at him as just a friend, so when we started dating a few years ago, I was still making that transition to viewing him as more. When Dick came on the scene with the agenda of collecting another wife, our relationship progressed towards marriage real fast. (Dick and I had met online, but we only became Facebook friends; he had actually come to a few parties of mine years prior, but there was no relationship. Then we started working on a blog together daily, and Dick showed interest in me within a couple of weeks and told me he's looking for a wife, not a girlfriend; he didn't want to date... so we actually started talking marriage from the beginning!) So I leveled with Stan, and he understood and was so gracious in letting me go. We didn't talk or text since then, until September 2014. Letting Stan go and marrying Dick was the biggest mistake of my life, because Stanton is absolutely wonderful <u>to me,</u> <u>with me</u> <u>and for me</u>! I had come up with these criteria when I was dating many years before. <u>A man can be good (in fact, this is only the primary requirement); but he has to be good to you (treatment); then good with you (compatibility and goals); then good for you (bringing out the best in you).</u> I believe I've found a "goalmate" in Stanton!]

*Yeah, I would have called him after my divorce, but as fate would have it, he emailed me four days after I filed! I responded, asking if it was from him, since it had only a link (like one of those group emails that are really spam from friends' hacked accounts). I also asked how he was, and what's new. He emailed back and confirmed that it was from him, and said he was fine; nothing new, and asked the same. I wrote back saying, "You won't believe what's new in my life!" He wrote back with much curiosity, so I indicated that he should call me. When I told him I had just filed for divorce, he asked me out! He wanted to go out that night, but I told him to at least let me get Dick served first! He said he wasn't going to wait and let another man snatch me* up again! Wow! That was so affirming – after a year of rejection from the very man who "snatched me up"! Stanton has been calling this past week. Wow!

I thank God; I did not set this up. I believe God allowed Stanton to contact me for such a time as this. It is so redeeming to have this happen with this timing! Stanton is like my "kinsmen redeemer", a Biblical concept. He was someone already connected to me, who was just meant to be, but I didn't know it. He had always been so good to me [prior to dating Dick], yet because I had always been looking to meet the "man of my dreams"... my "soulmate", I had not realized that my need was really for a goalmate. And how sweet it is for a "solid friend" of your past to end up being the boyfriend and goalmate of your future!

### "IT IS IDEAL TO KEEP IT REAL!"

I don't believe in expectations like, "God will send me the 'man of my dreams'" anymore. Many women do get the man of their dreams, but it seems that most don't. Even in lasting marriages, he may not be her "dream" guy, but he is a great guy and great husband! Even for those who may start out with their "dream" guy, at some point that changes or the women change their perspective of that fantasy "man of my dreams" concept. I think it's alright to desire and look for that, but at the same time realize that holding out for that might not be practical. Everybody doesn't get everything in life. Some people don't even get mates, much less, dream mates! I'd rather have a great man in my life than hold out year after year, decade after decade for the "man of my dreams"!

If you think about it, dreams aren't real, so in some respects, you're looking for an "unreal" man! You're actually looking for a "made-up" man... a figment of your imagination! No wonder so many relationships end up in disillusion; you're finally seeing straight at that point! You're finally "awake", not in a dream! Maybe Hollywood played a number on us. But I think we do enough dreaming on our own, without the help of Hollywood. I believe we need to keep it real! No more conjuring up "unreal" images of men of our dreams. Have a list of ideals, but keep it real!

## Chapter 12: WHY SO MAD?

*October 3rd, 2014 (cont'd)*

*I often wonder why he is so mad at me. What did I do? He has never, ever told me what I did in our marriage that he had a problem with. The only thing he ever stated was that he didn't like my expectation that he eat dinner when he gets home, because he felt that I was controlling him. While I thought I was doing a wonderful, "wifely" thing... to have a hot meal waiting for him, he thought that it was a controlling thing, and resented it. So I stopped! He's never shared another thing that I've done. The night in May when I asked him if he'd go to counseling with me, and he agreed, I asked again, what problem he is having with me. He wouldn't tell me, and said he'll say it in the counseling session! I asked, "Why not tell me before we even needed counseling?" He said it was because of the way that I take things. I asked how he could know how I take things, since he's never shared anything for me to "take" any certain way! He had no response. And at the counseling session in June, he couldn't come up with anything! When the counselor gave him the floor several times to voice his concerns, in deep concentration and with much delay, all he could come up with was that we don't seem to have musical and movie interests in common.*

*Wow! We had sooooo much in common before we were married; so was he faking it back then? We had our Christian-walk in common, church going, Rev. class, Chicago Steppin' classes, walks in Claremont, movies, music, politics, intellectually stimulating conversation, loving extended periods of kissing, massages, etc.*

*So, after several attempts to pull something out of him, the counselor moved on, and then much later, Dick blurted out something; like he just thought of something that might seem a bit more substantial. He said that "Janice is quite a few years older than I am, and so I think she acts like she's my mother!" Dick didn't elaborate, so the counselor and I saw that it was just a cheap shot.*

*So, why is he so mad? Why was he so resistant when we were married? What did I do? Was it because I became privy to his ED secret? Resultantly, when that secret was out, he tried to condition me to accept that secret, which meant that he had to mistreat me and see if I'd stick through the mistreatment.*

I think it's deeper than that. He had been in denial about his ED. I believe his anger was because I confirmed his fear that he really did have erectile dysfunction. I think he thought that his impotence would be cured by sex once married! Counterintuitive, I know! But I think he thought that since he had been attracted to me, that once married and able to indulge, he'd be able to; he'd "rise" to the occasion... pun intended!

Then at that point when it didn't rise, was he mad because he had to come to the realization that he possibly couldn't be aroused by a woman? Or, maybe his conflict was over whether or not he was even still attracted to women. I say this because before marriage, he really seemed into me and attracted to me. Well, when it didn't rise, I believe he started questioning whether or not he was truly attracted to me (or to women). Then, to save face, he convinced himself that he wasn't attracted to me, and had to convince me that he wasn't.

*He certainly was displaying no attraction to me – even in the first month of marriage! I could walk in front of him naked, and he'd have no facial response. I could put on sexy lingerie, but no facial reaction! Even one month into our marriage [I allude to "birthday sex" in a flashback], he was already trying to "condition" me not to believe that there was sexual interest or desire. This was to keep me at bay, so there'd be no pressure on him.*

<u>Then, I think because he didn't see himself as attracted to me, he felt trapped in an unwanted marriage.</u> He resented me for not being the woman I should be; a woman who could arouse him! <u>There are so many psychological dynamics involved when a man has ED!</u> It is so much more than physical! And it impacts the wife so much more than just the lack of intercourse. What he put me through because of the ED was so much worse than the ED! So, was his anger towards me because I wasn't someone who could make it rise to have sex? So, was it my fault? And so in his mind, did he find himself trapped in a sexless marriage because of me... because I didn't arouse him?

*No wonder he was so relieved to go when I stated that we must separate. Was he thinking about getting with a person who could arouse him? Did he have a "person" in mind?*

I believe his anger towards me throughout the marriage points to another dynamic. If he were truly struggling with his sexual identity before we got together – yet he decided to marry me to prove otherwise – and yet I didn't allow him to accomplish his objective by arousing him past his ED to have sex with a female – then he was left prone to this asexual or other possibility! Sex with a woman... could he take it or leave it? And if I'm questioning it, it's a strong possibility that he's questioning it. I believe he is. He always brought up something peculiar to me. He would frequently bring up the term, "metrosexual", and I would wonder why. It would always be in reference to other men whom he deemed as metrosexual; I don't remember him defining himself as such. I'd always wonder why it was important to him to mention that. Another thing that he brought up on several occasions was that when he was a young adult, he had turned down a sexual advance from a man. I think he was making sure, just in case I wondered, that he was not heterosexual. But this backfired. It made me think that he was planting this information for that very reason. Those times that I'd ask him what's wrong, why he isn't talking to me, why he is aloof – he wasn't going to articulate this! No wonder he kept me in the dark about what problems he had with me!

*Boy, I stepped into some sh--!!!! This stuff is deep! I didn't deserve this! And I'm not blaming God. I will write about it for other women to read and learn from. I will share not only what went on, but I'll share the bigger picture – the possible root issues, which are more universal than my actual scenarios.*

Back to the question about his anger, I also wonder why it was present last month when I saw him. It's obvious. Because I had asked him to pay up the month prior to that, and he had no intentions! But why an angry response instead of just avoidance? Was it because he was "found out"? Because he was put on notice? His cover was blown? The real "good-guy" was found to be a fraud? This is enough to anger him. His reputation of being this great guy with integrity is his greatest asset; and to have it blown like that uncovers him! It's enough to make a nice guy mad!

## Chapter 13: <u>DEDICATED TO DEDICATION</u>

*Tuesday, October 7$^{th}$, 2014*

*On Sunday night, 10/5, Jeanine [my daughter] took me out to a movie. When I saw previews that intrigued me, I subconsciously thought about how I'd like to see this movie* and that movie with Dick; how we'd both enjoy this subject matter and that! I had to check myself! I was really transported back 1.5 years ago, when we used to date and enjoy movies together! We were so on one accord; we really enjoyed doing things together... experiencing things together. We were such a united pair; we really appeared to be soulmates. It felt sooo good, and so real, and so right! I really miss him. But I miss "the him" I thought he was! The "him" he portrayed himself to be back then. But that was a fictitious "him"! That "him" didn't really exist! Because within months of those great memories that we made, he hustled me out of money, then kept on throughout the marriage (not to mention the ED fraud!!)!!

## FINANCIAL FRAUD FLASHBACK

The hustle began with the engagement. By the time we needed to have announced our engagement and been inviting people to our wedding initially planned for August 2013, we still were not engaged. He had just gotten a temporary job in May, and claimed he had no means of paying for the ring, because after paying rent, he had only $400 of income left for food, gas and bills. So we pushed the wedding date back to September and eliminated the ceremony. [It was a private beach wedding without family.] Then, when the end of July was upon us and he continued to claim he couldn't afford the ring yet, we decided we'd just purchase the ring with my money, and he'd pay me back once his positon became permanent; which he claimed his employer said was imminent!

*He defrauded me out of that money by never paying me back; but the scam came in the lying from the beginning! I only realized this much later, due to his later claim that his parents had been paying his rent those months he'd claimed he was paying it! He actually got to keep that $1,200 per month from May until September, so he really could have purchased my ring! What a liar! And telling me that he wanted to get me an expensive ring "that my friends would be jealous of"... he really played me!*

*Another instance of my realization of his premeditated deception and intent not to repay me for my ring was this: The day that we were to have returned to the jewelry store for me to purchase his wedding band of choice, he showed up with the band! I was surprised, and I reminded him that I was going to buy his ring, just as I had expected that he purchase mine. I asked him why he had done that. His response was evasive; back then I didn't know that his M.O. was evasion coupled with deception. He ran out and bought his ring so he could say that he bought his own ring, and I bought my own! He had it planned from the beginning!*

## PERCEPTION DECEPTION

*So, sometimes I have to remind myself not to think fondly of Dick, because he was a fraud from the beginning! I cannot afford to "miss him", because the "him" I miss never actually existed!*

That's a distinction that women really need to make. Sometimes a woman keeps going back to her man who's wronged her, because of the fond memories of the life they had together based on her perception of him. But if that perception is fallacious, then the relationship is built on and being sustained by figments of her imagination. In these cases, you are devoted to the memories, not a real relationship. And so you fill in the gaps to have a continuum of good memories. So when something just isn't right, you manage to overlook those things or make excuses for them or for him. And the things that are overt – not just gray areas – you forgive and forget, because... isn't that what we're supposed to do for any loved one?

But we must always be honest with ourselves about what's really going on, and <u>our dedication to that person must be commensurate. Otherwise, we are expressing devotion to a man who has an "agenda" that doesn't really include our welfare. He may treat you decently some, or even most of the time, but when the time comes that your welfare and his agenda don't match, then one suffers... and it's usually you.</u>

## SECRET AGENDAS

*Tuesday, October 7th, 2014 (cont'd)*

Think about it. Things can go along fine for a while, but then there are those confusing behaviors that are out of sync with whom he has projected himself to be. You dismiss them, but the same type of situation keeps arising. That's not by coincidence. They are based on his (or her) will to make things go according to his secret agenda. His agenda usually arises out of being self-serving, manifesting in anything from greed to fraud to infidelity.

[Expounding on the greed and fraud agendas, there is actually a name for a sick group of men out there who prey on mature, established women. They are called "Sophistication Pimps"! They seek out sophisticated ladies who unknowingly finance their living, businesses, etc. Beware!]

Or, this "secret agenda" might even be a secret to him, in which case, I call it "faulty-wiring". He may be totally unaware of his faulty way of looking at things; he could have picked these ways up from watching his parents! Or, it could be an unchecked train of thought that had served him well when he was single, but is fatal to a marriage.

Case in point: Dick came from a supportive household from the beginning, and I have tremendous admiration for his parents. They put three young men through college, and even in Dick's 40's, his parents were paying his rent and living expenses when he lost his job. Then, even once he got a job, since his pay was low, he said they continued paying his rent. This framed his point of view on the level of financial commitment a parent should have towards their children... even as adults. So, when he had four kids of his own, he had the same level of commitment, and that's fine. Dick is very committed to his offspring, and I applaud that. But when he married me and generated charges to my credit card, when it came time to pay those charges, he refused payment, always telling me that his children needed money (this is over and above child support).

This is wrong, but he thinks it's right, based on his strongly anchored views of parental financial obligation. So this was his secret agenda, which could have even been subconscious as is faulty-wiring; having picked it up since childhood. He literally admitted in our only counseling session two weeks before our separation, that he didn't think that he should have had to contribute to our household... that I was paying all the bills before he got there, so why should he have to pay half of them! So he fought me month after month just about contributing towards half the bills! I will always remember him telling me that that was his money! The money he earned was his, not mine! So his secret agenda was to avoid any financial matters with me... period!

Perhaps I can site this as another reason why Dick seemed put off by me. He thought I was "taking money from his kids"! The money that he spent on our household – he could have been spending on his other households! That's what he meant when he expressed his distorted viewpoint, that he shouldn't have to pay bills in our household. He thought he could just "tip" me now and then by paying an electric bill now and then. Well, this would definitely explain why he was mad at me. I stood in the way of his agenda to spend all his resources on his other households. He resented this. He fought me every month when bills were due, both HHX and CC debt. This secret agenda was a cancer eating away at our marriage. Either I was going to let it metathesize by getting further and further into debt, or I was going to surgically remove it. I chose the latter!

So, back to the commensurate comment; my response had to align itself with what was actually happening. Fighting every month wasn't solving it. I had to put my foot down; I had to stop the financial drain, not to mention the other huge problem. Women who don't take action against those secret agendas or faulty-wiring fall prey to emotional abuse or worse: depression, financial ruin, and of course just an unhappy marriage.

### CANCEL HIS AGENDA!

A proper response to the circumstance is key. But instead, a very common response to those times that we know that he isn't doing right by us is to nag. I think that's why we hear this as a common complaint from men. However, this is because we feel powerless to the real culprit, which is sometimes difficult to pinpoint, especially if it is his secret agenda. We may feel the power of our hollering, arguing, wrath or nagging, so we substitute these responses for the corrective, commensurate power response. But none of these substitutes cancels the secret agenda. To that, we are still defenseless, until we identify and address it head on, taking the necessary, corresponding, commensurate action.

Let your nagging be a signal that there is an underlying problem that you must confront head on. Nagging from a woman is like whining from a child. A child is having a problem with an action from his parent, yet he is defenseless, so he whines. A wife is having a problem brought on by the secret agenda of her husband, yet she is defenseless (either because she hasn't identified the secret agenda, or she doesn't feel empowered to take action against it), so she nags. Nagging only gets us labeled, and it doesn't get us corrective behavior. We really must take corrective action! By position, a child is defenseless against actions of his parents; so childish responses are expected of a child. But a wife should never be defenseless in her relationship, nor should a husband. It is supposed to be a partnership, with him as the head, not as the autocrat. Identify the culprit, address it, and if it doesn't change, take corrective action.

Sometimes we do the opposite of nagging; we internalize and suppress the issue to keep the relationship afloat. We are so dedicated to being dedicated that we allow unhealthy behavior to continue. Out of my dedication to the marriage, I attempted to suppress my needs by staying with this man who had defrauded me from the beginning. Out of devotion to him, I suppressed my sexual needs, because for ten months, this man never once had his ED problem addressed by a diabetes specialist. So, my devotion wasn't commensurate with his! He wasn't even devoted to trying to have a sexual relationship with his wife! Nor was he devoted to supporting his household. Nor was he even devoted to his health! So if I had kept on with my incommensurate response of devotion to his blatant disrespect to the financial and sexual health of our marriage, then I would have just ended up broken and bitter! And aren't these the two adjectives that often describe women in relationships? Either broken, bitter or both (BBB)!

## NEW RULES!

Well, don't become a BBB! Make your responses and your level of devotion commensurate with reality. It is not a call to play games. It is a call to end his game playing! You have to know you're in a game; then you have to know the rules of the game; then you have to change the rules of the game or quit the game! <u>If you don't know the rules of the game, you lose by default!</u>

The rules that he had set up in my case had been that he resists and resents me when it comes to contributing to the household. My responses had been that of confusion and anxiety. The rules regarding sex were that I get none. He'd break me off a bit of foreplay maybe twice a month; but don't you dare expect more! So my response was to suppress my desires. I thought that to love him, I had to show devotion by pressing through my anxiety and suppressing my needs. I thought that devotion equaled putting up with the crap... status quo! But then I realized that, just as I should be "grateful but not content", I should be "devoted but not complacent"!

Love and devotion don't give him a license to taking advantage or abuse. Call it tough love; waking up and smelling the coffee; letting your response be commensurate with the action; or changing the rules of the game. You can love the man, but hate the actions. You should love the man, but require the health of your marriage! You should not nag or suppress, but plan a course of action commensurate with his actions. In my case, taking action was to "restart the game with new rules"; to "push the reset button" on our marriage with a separation with a purpose [then divorce]. I stopped the financial bleeding. Taking action also meant adopting the stance that it is not alright to have a marriage without even trying to fix the impotence issue.

Taking action is like when you make the decision to give your child what she needs rather than what she wants. You know that it will be best in the end, and that she'll ultimately appreciate it more. <u>It may feel like taking action is giving up on the relationship. But it is actually a statement of love and devotion. And it's a devotion to the ultimate health of the marriage, not to the short term desires of just one of the two. Devotion is long-termed. Devotion by definition infers that you're committed to doing what's going to make it last. That means the elimination of those factors that won't let it last. You can't be devoted to something that you know is not sustainable; so taking the right action steps is strategic to sustainability! Being complacent with any status-quo unhealthy circumstances destroys any hopes of sustainability. Change the rules; take action!</u>

*Changing the rules in my case was to "reset" our relationship and to establish boundaries. I still loved Dick and wanted to see us get back to how we were pre-marriage. It seemed in our case that the only time that things were really right was in our pre-marriage days [so I thought]. That's because sex and finances were not an issue back then. I just wish that we had stayed in that state. I would still have my friend. We would also still be physically closer than we ever were when married, because all the affection stopped once his ED issue was exposed. We would make plans to go to some of those movies that I saw trailers for. We would still be going out dancing! I would still think the world of him. We would still be in love! I wish that we had just never married. It would have still been good. And if you think of it, the two things that should have gotten better as a married couple never happened anyway! We should have been able to merge expenses and thus save money, and we should have been able to draw physically closer through a sex life; but that didn't happen either! So, we would have been better off just dating or just friends! And, if we had just dated long enough, maybe some of his secrets would have come out, and we could have dealt with them through counseling and medical intervention. Maybe one day in the future, these issues would have become resolved, and we would have had a successful happy marriage then. And most of all, I never would have had to know that he could spitefully use me and defraud me.*

[In editing this book in February 2016, I look at this last paragraph in awe! I so am over it! I don't wish for any type of relationship with Dick, and haven't since I wrote that! Back then, I was still thinking that things just got in the way; the timing wasn't right. Wrong! <u>The man wasn't right!</u>

<u>The timing is never right with the wrong man.</u> He scammed me, and after a year and a half, he has never tried to make monetary restitution. So he would have been no kind of real friend, even had we never married and had I never been used. He still had it in him. He's a user! Interesting how back then I could still have some misappropriated thoughts about him – incongruent with whom he really was. Ladies, sometimes it takes some time!]

## WISE COUNSEL

*Tuesday, October 7$^{th}$, 2014 (cont'd)*

Some people are in your life for just a season; therefore, you need to go through at least a full cycle of seasons to determine his reason. Time may tell that his reason for his season in your life was just for his gain. On the other hand, you can have the right match, but if you haven't put in the time, you can't expect to make the "discoveries" that you could work on prior to the marriage, giving your marriage the best shot. This is the reason that I am now a big advocate of long-termed dating and even long engagements. You need to give sufficient time to determine that they are who they say they are! That is because people with secret agendas can hide them much better in short-termed courtships, like Dick did. And even if a long courtship unveils some secrets, through counseling and hard work, some issues can be successfully resolved. These issues should be resolved prior to any engagement, however, and some issues are just deal breakers.

So, pre-marital counseling is the other opportunity for discoveries. Had Dick and I gotten counseling, we would have discussed finances and perhaps would have unveiled his misguided sense of household responsibility (his faulty-wiring). Any counselor would have known that his views were displaced and lethal to a marriage. Last August, when I informed Dr. Z. of our separation, he concluded the same thing. He said that if Dick would allow him to counsel us, he would point out this fallacy. Pre-marital counseling would have been best, obviously, and it should always include deep honest conversations about plans for money.

[While reviewing my memoir, I felt that I should expound on this point. These deep honest conversations have to be designed to uncover not only plans for money, but also to make discoveries about each other's actual financial situations; you don't want to walk into any liabilities. Your partner may owe substantial sums of money to other parties, but you wouldn't know it. And even if he makes payments on those sums himself, without involving your income, it will still impact the money available to your household.

So make sure when choosing your counselor, that he or she has modules directed towards financial "discoveries and disclosures". Even having dated for a long time, there is usually no easy way to say to your loved one, "Let me see your pay stubs, tax returns, child support records and credit reports." But your counselor can and should say it! Both parties should lay it out there; if there are back taxes, outstanding child support, debt, defaults, or if any liens exist, the other party will be apprised. <u>This advice is especially true for people about to get married later in life, who have either amassed assets or liabilities; you need to position yourself to protect your assets, because he may be about to position himself to become your liability!</u>

For this reason, couples at this stage of life should retain title to their own mortgages; if one party sells their home to move in with their spouse, then they should agree that this money belongs to that party. It is also practical for couples to agree to keep their own bank account and investment information private, but to agree upon sums toward the household budget. This is especially true of mature couples who will want to pass their assets down to their own children or grandchildren... not to an ex in a divorce battle. Be fair to your posterity. Use wisdom... I didn't. My mistake was in circumventing both "discovery" phases. I didn't date him for long enough, and I didn't get pre-marital counseling.]

### Chapter 14: "WORSE THAN AN INFIDEL!"

*Tuesday, October 7<sup>th</sup>, 2014 (cont'd)*

*It is interesting to think that had we waited another year and gone through counseling sessions, how we could have had a different outcome. In fact, we wouldn't have been under the time and money crunch for the wedding, so my fronting the money for the ring never would have come into play. So, the monster that I see now may have never raised his ugly head had we taken it slowly, gone to counseling, and had I and made him take financial responsibility for this new bride he was seeking and the new household he was seeking to establish. But no, I had to "help" him when his funds were low!*

This says a lot about women trying to help their men. We want to be helpful and show that we have their backs. But men just don't seem to fair well when their women are in the position to "help" them, because that means that their women are doing better than they are, and that's a problem of its own! Some men just can't take it, so they act out in other ways – they take advantage.

2 Thessalonians 3:10 says that, "If a man doesn't work, he shouldn't eat." This is a profound statement; God knows it's a real intrinsic issue when a man doesn't take care of his own household. So much so, that God goes on to say in 1 Timothy 5:8, "A man who doesn't take care of his household is worse than an infidel!" Something happens in the mind of a man who does not work for what he wants and does not pay his own way. He loses his manliness, and as a husband, loses his sense of wanting to be a provider. Instead, he becomes the opposite – a user! <u>And in that state, a wife and a mother kind of look the same!</u> In fact, many men marry their moms! This statement means that they look for someone, or are attracted to someone who can take care of them as their mother did. Unfortunately, I did, by advancing him money.

It can also mean that this woman has traits and characteristics or the personality of their mom. Dick often told me that I remind him of his mom. At that time, I didn't know the significance of those statements! When I had shared with Pastor Ken about my farcical marriage, he concluded that Dick had married his mom! He wanted a stable giving woman who'd be his caretaker. Wow! That's some true insight! I may have reminded Dick of his mom, the woman, but he used me as his mom, the provider!

*But there were signs pointing to the fact that he was already a user and that he had a dependent relationship with his mom. So there was a compounding effect. I noticed when we were dating, that he'd let me give him money when I knew he didn't have gas money, or when we were out on a free date (that's how we did it), but got hungry and needed to stop somewhere. I also had a product that I sold, and when he'd accompany me to sell it, I'd give him half of my earnings for coming. But before we dated I had sold by myself, so it's not like he added anything to the sales! But I'm generous, and he knew that!*

*Well, I noticed these things, but didn't have a frame of reference for categorizing it. And although he didn't work, he was looking for work... but he had to eat. In this economy, sometimes it takes years to find another job, I rationalized. But there were plenty of sales positions he threw away because he didn't want to do sales! His parents were paying his way, and his girlfriend was feeding him [lunch and dinner, daily!], so he didn't have to take the jobs. Thus, he wasn't working... but he was eating!*

Both his parents and I violated that biblical principle, and hence, contributed to his misconception that he didn't have to take care of his household. Hence, he had become worse than an infidel... even prior to our marriage when he lied about his finances. I married an impotent infidel!

The word "infidel" means a person who doesn't believe in Christ. In fact, a different translation uses the phrase, "has denied the faith and is worse than an unbeliever." Although Dick professes Christ with his mouth, his actions betray that, according to God's word. Through his actions, he has effectually denied the faith, and is worse than someone who never received Christ. Therefore, he can spout off at the mouth about his faith, teach Bible studies, etc., but his actions pretty much reveal that he really isn't a follower of Christ in spirit! An infidel!

Women should be careful about "helping" our men financially. We hinder them and aid and abet in the abandonment of his manly responsibilities. Remember that, as men, many of them are just leaving boyhood and taking on manhood. Don't send them back into boyhood by, unbeknownst to you, becoming their mom! You know how some women joke about having three kids; two offspring and their husbands make the third! As Pastor Ken says, they joke about it, but over time, it becomes a painful reality, and something that can tear away at the marriage. Let's find other ways to become "helpmeets" for our husbands other than financial.

*In counseling me, Pastor Ken said that Dick thrived on the combination of independent factors that ultimately culminated in the scenario where he could deceive me. In other words, it was the "perfect storm"! He was the victim of an economy where good educated people endured long periods of unemployment; yet he had parents supporting him and a generous woman feeding him and giving him pocket change. And the wind in this perfect storm was the fact that he took a temp agency job, anticipating his wages to increase with the imminent permanent position. And the ominous cloud in this storm was the goal to have a quick wedding before his daughter went off to college. All this pointed to my funds to the rescue! It was the perfect storm for my getting suckered in! He played it well and reaped the benefits! He's an opportunist; which is just another name for "user"!*

*I won't date men who have less than I do anymore! They must have their own money, have a passport, and even a nicer car! Why a nicer car? Because I've even had a date to tell me that my BMW intimidated him! Can't have that! I used* to say that I wanted to build and grow together with my man; therefore, he didn't have to have it all. But now I see how that can turn out. I'm going to say something that can be misconstrued... but to a degree, "gold-diggers" have it right! They know that the secret is to marry up, not down! They're wrong for using men, but they are at least safeguarding themselves from being used.

OVER TEN PAGES LATER!

*Tuesday, October 7<sup>th</sup>, 2014 (cont'd)*

Wow! Several pages later, I get back to my initial entry! [But that's the beauty of journaling! It is a means of expressing thoughts that you had not yet articulated; it is cathartic, and it is also an opportunity for the Holy Spirit to download truths to you. I highly recommend it! In fact, while the Holy Spirit downloaded truths to me about my circumstances, He also downloaded general truths as a message to you ladies, via my published journal! Thank you, God!]

Movies really did prompt this feeling of missing him. But this is only because I missed my movie watching buddy... not the fraudulent man himself. The previews made me consider how I've lost my movie watching buddy for good, plus all the other lost opportunities with my former close companion. This all reminded me of the movie, "The Notebook", which made me ponder the issue of true love. The love story was told through the eyes of an old man to his nursing home companion who was demented. She didn't even remember that she was his wife, and that the story was theirs. He was so crushed that he couldn't have her as his wife anymore, due to her loss of memory. But he was soooo devoted to her that he left their home to live in the facility with her.

I considered the pain he felt over his loss, and tried to console myself into believing that I'm better off having never had a long-term true love, than suffering the loss. That pain that he portrayed was so real that I wept. I'm tearing now! I won't have to have that pain, because nobody has ever loved me enough to where a loss would be so devastating! Do I even still want that kind of love? I don't know. I know that I used to, but I'm not so sure now. It kind of goes back to... at this point in my life, I don't want to hold out for my "soulmate"; I'd rather proceed with my "goalmate" with whom to step into our "next chapter".

## BIRTHDAY-BUZZ

Sunday, October 19th, 2014

It's my birthday! I'm fifty-five! 55 years old! I'm in my mid-50's; middle aged! I confess it and embrace it! And I thank God for it! It was a glorious day! Jeremy and Jeanine went to church with me and then took me to the best brunch! The food is sooooo tasty at Pomona Valley Mining Company, and the hilltop view is fabulous! I enjoyed myself immensely with my kids! They are so crazy! Then, Jeanine took me to get a massage. Real nice! Stanton will take me to a play next week.

*Then, I got a birthday-wish call from a friend who gave me great insights into Dick after I told him of our status. He knows someone who had gone to church with Dick and had told him some things about Dick. He said Dick had a very nasty, public divorce. Their whole church knew of it, and it's a mighty big church. He made the comment that maybe something in our marriage prompted that response in him. Confused, I asked what could have prompted him to refuse to cover his own living expenses. He clarified that maybe something in the marriage reminded him of something in his former marriage, thus he responded accordingly.*

*This rang true! I had always thought that his responses to me sounded like he was picking up from a conversation he'd had with another! He'd say, "I'm not standing for this!" I'd always wonder, "Stand for what?" He'd escalate the conversation to argument level real fast, and I'd just stand in amazement, wondering what happened! Any conversation where he was asked to do something he didn't want to, like paying bills, would trigger odd responses!*

*He has unresolved issues with his ex-wife! I got real confirmation on my own suspicions; real insight! And hearing how they blew out in public, I can see that his issues are so deep that he hasn't had time for the wounds to heal. Any woman would get his wrath! That's probably why his mom had told him that he should never get married again. She knew that the unresolved problems with his ex would impact his next! He has real women issues!*

## Chapter 15: HE'S NOT THE PRIZE!

*Tuesday, October 21st, 2014*

I am at a place in my life, where I don't consider a "husband" to be a prize. So many Christian women have beliefs that God will reward their faithfulness with a husband. And especially if their faithfulness included abstinence; then God owed them the desire of their heart – a good husband! Many of these women of whom I speak are over 50 and still holding on to this belief. I personally know many women who have never been married before, and some of them have abstained from sexual relations for most of their adult lives, awaiting their "prinze"... their "prince-prize"!

I was one of those abstinent women for many years. I really thought that there was no way that God wouldn't "bless me with a husband"; after all, I was depriving myself of one of the most natural and basic human functions that He created! But I don't think that God meant for us to deprive ourselves of any basic function for years and decades! It would be just like if I had deprived myself of solid food for years on end! Imagine, just trying to be content with shakes, soups and smoothies, knowing that there are fruits, veggies, seafood, meat, BBQ, pasta, casseroles, desserts, etc. to enjoy! And to what avail? No one said that if we deprive ourselves of solid food, we'd get some prize; and no one said that if we deprived ourselves of pre-marital sex, we'd get the "prize" of a "husband"! We Christian women want to think that. Standing on the scripture that "He will give us the desires of our hearts" (Psalms 37:4), we even give Him our wish list; we put in our orders.

Yet, there are so many women who don't "get a husband"; the desire of their hearts! There are so many reasons why some women never meet their mate. Maybe it's because we've been sold on the dream of a "soulmate", instead of the ideal of a "goalmate"! Perhaps it is the "eligible bachelor odds"... the modern day dating dilemma. But since we know that it only takes meeting one guy... the right guy, we think of the odds as not that bad. "Surely, one man, out of all the men I run into will be husband material and compatible with me," we keep thinking!

And so we go about our encounters with men with expectations of God having "planted" the right kind of guy in our paths. So, we meet a guy, and we ask ourselves, "Could this be the one?" And we give him too much access to our lives, thinking that after all, "this could be of God!" Then we spend too much time with someone with whom we should never have been in a relationship in the first place. We have over-spiritualized it and given the "relationship" credence when it never should have even taken place. In fact, in the natural, we never would have even dated some of these guys. But since in our eagerness we "spiritualize" things, we believe that God in His omniscience could have sent this guy! After all, He knows whom we need better than we do. So, we give that guy too much of our time before we conclude that he "can't" be of God. Then, we keep praying that, "God, send me my husband" prayer, which again, heightens our expectation of meeting our husband. So then we give another man access to our lives who was never meant to be. In fact, I can point to many men whom I really would not have dated were it not for my telling myself that I had to be open to what God might have in store for me. Since what He has for me might not even be on my "list", I must keep an open mind and therefore give the person in front of me a chance.

It even got to the point where I thought that every man that I met was possibly from God. <u>I should have realized that, since it takes only one – the right one – God doesn't have to keep sending many!</u> I had one of those "Aha!" moments where a girlfriend had to check me. I recall relaying to her how things went awry with a guy whom I had been dating, and I said, "I wonder why God even let me meet him!" Shocked at my statement, she said, "You're going to meet many men as you go about life, but that doesn't mean that God sent them!" Well, she was certainly right, and it jeered me back into reality. I had been living in that world of "God will put me in the right place at the right time to meet the right man" for so long, that for me, it translated into – wherever I was, if I met a man (because meeting new men was so rare for me), I automatically thought that God was up to something! That thinking got me into less than ideal relationships for a long time; so it was time to change my thinking. [But it's apparent that I didn't...]

But since I've heard this line of thinking from many other women as well, I believe that there's a message in this for women in general. We as women need to check ourselves. We think that God's "blessing of a husband" will happen in serendipitous ways and so we fill in the blanks to any circumstance and write a fairytale encounter and ending. Or even worse, if we believe that it is of God, we don't spend enough time in the "relationship" before deciding to get married! This was my mistake... twice! I figured that if God is up to something, He surely can complete it; it doesn't take my human interjection of "time" into it. We can just complete the union with marriage and live happily ever after. And especially if we've been abstinent (which was the case both times), then God will surely bless it! God will "surely honor" our union, because we "did it the right way!" Well, it didn't happen that way... twice!

## Chapter 16: "GOD DUST"

*Tuesday, October 21$^{st}$, 2014 (cont'd)*

This is that fairytale kind of thinking; we get "living by the spirit" and "living by faith" mixed up with fairytales! Living by the spirit and by faith doesn't mean that we're not to live out our earthly lives using earthly principles. Earthly principles of time and space still apply! Earthly principles of using your mind are actually honored by God. He gives us volitional minds, meaning that He allows us to make up our own minds about anything in life. He does not stop us in our decisions. He may warn us and direct us, but He does not stop us or make us. We want this freedom. We'd be puppets otherwise. We enjoy our freedom to be who we want to be and to behave as we choose.

Now, even if we do choose to align ourselves with God's will and way, He doesn't put our will and our way on autopilot. We still have daily decisions to make. But here's where we get lazy. We hope that since we're on "Team Jesus", He'll set up our circumstances for us – especially to send us good husbands. Instead of putting in the work and enough time, we hope that God will sprinkle "God Dust" on our situation and our relationship to make it a good union. No; that was "Tinker Bell" who sprinkled "fairy dust"! But we're not living in that fairytale! So in our "real lives", what we're not factoring in is that – even if we surrender our will to His, and even if we're so in-tune with the Holy Spirit that our daily decisions are made by Him – decisions made by our significant other will still affect us! We're not in a bubble. And God doesn't sprinkle "God Dust" on our relational situations to make all the outcomes right! We still have to make our own decisions, and our partner makes his! God guides and leads, but we either choose or refuse His leading; we still have to call our shots, and our partner calls his – good or bad! And our partner's bad shots will affect us! So a good thing can go sour.

But even if we call good shots and our partner calls bad ones, God can and does work according to Romans 8:28: "And we know that all things work together for good to them that love God, to them who are the called according to his purpose." But this verse applies to the outcomes after either party has called a bad shot that affects the other! So there is no "God Dust" to insure that nothing goes wrong in our relationship choices, but there is God's assurance that He is still in control.

*I believe that in many cases, God does bring a potential mate into our lives. But at some point, before or after marriage, that mate can allow his volitional mind to take a series of actions contrary to the health of that relationship (and so can you). Then we wonder what went wrong and if God really did have anything to do with that union. In my case, I wondered why God even allowed the relationship to continue towards marriage, even with no red-flags about the two big culprits. God knew that my spouse was impotent; had no desire to financially contribute to his new household; and would defraud me financially in order to keep his money to himself. Why would God allow this union? I prayed for God's guidance on our union, and I believed I got His green-light. I even got "Word of Knowledge" confirmations from Christians. I had never had people share their visions over me like that before, but to have these confirmations in addition to my prayers seemed to be more than enough confirmation. Either way, I was more than happy to add it to all the reasons we should get married!*

[I want to expound on this now. Before Dick and I were even dating, a wonderful lady at Rev. class looked at my guest, Dick, and asked if he was my husband. She wasn't asking was I married; she was asking was that the man I'm married to. Both of us were stumped, because we could tell that she was speaking from a vision. When she realized that we weren't married and that her vision was of a future event, not current, she changed the subject. But we let this influence us. We added it to our supposed confirmations that God had put this together.

At this point, after our divorce, I still wonder what that was all about! I've heard people who get visions from God say that they can't always tell the context of the vision; whether it is future or present. So obviously with her vision, it was future. But the question is, why would God give me a doomed marriage and give her that vision that made us think it was meant to be?

Although I don't have the answer to this spiritual question yet, let me go back to the natural. We all make decisions, good or bad. I obviously made a bad one; God didn't choose Dick for me. God knew that this man was never able or willing to have a sex life with his wife, or to even pay for his own living expenses. This is not a husband. But since I didn't know this about him, I made the mistake of marrying him. Well, as a prophetess, she had this vision of the marriage that we did have in the future. But her vision was not to imply that God put this marriage together! It just meant that it would happen and she saw it! But Christians tend to spiritualize things and so we all thought it meant a God-ordained, sanctioned marriage!

Look at the many prophesies in the Bible. They were visions of things that would happen, but that doesn't mean that all these things that would happen were going to be good! Some were bad! But they happened! Well our marriage was bad; but it happened! Lesson learned!

I will also add that I've had two others "speak into my life", and I look expectantly to the fulfillment of those visions! At different times, both Pastor Ken and Pastor Wade of my church, POG, have told me that they see me being an extremely successful business person in the future. So... I'm working on that! Now, back to my premise:]

If we're to live out our marriage on earth, then we need to apply some earthly principles and parameters. But don't get it twisted! I didn't say "worldly"; I said "earthly". "Worldly" things are considered not of God. But "earthly" things were created by God! He created the earth, the physical principles that govern this earth, and our minds with which to comprehend and successfully navigate our lives on this earth!

With our minds, God expects us to use reasoning and discernment to make good decisions; everyone doesn't hear from the Holy Spirit, who gives guidance, but everyone was given minds. So when seeking marriage, it is important to discern if we're right for each other. We're told to have prospect lists of "must haves" and "desires". If we find ourselves in a relationship with someone we like, but who isn't a list-fit, we should use our discernment. Maybe, put in perspective, some of those areas are really non-issues, or maybe they should remain on our lists as deal-breakers.

My problem was that I had assumed that God put some of my deal-breakers on my non-issues list. For instance, on my list was a man who had no minors. But the man who pursued me with an interest in marriage had three minors. So I rationalized that if God had put us together, then He'd sprinkle "God Dust" on it, and it would become a non-issue. I had not yet discovered the goalmate principle based on stages of life. Dick's stage of life was raising minors. Mine was "next chapter", so it wasn't an ideal match for me (for others whose goals are different, it could be an ideal match). But I thought that I saw my "soulmate" in him, and so I abandoned reason for an ethereal concept.

I put my "spiritual hat" on and buried my "earth-realm hat". But guess what... I got an earthly divorce, didn't I? At some point, I had to interject the earthly realm. Well, I should have done this sooner. I should have thought with the mind that God gave me instead of defaulting to what I thought was a spiritual response, which actually abdicated the responsibility of earthly discernment. Yes, pray and wait for a response, yet use discernment and reason. I shouldn't have put my mind up on a shelf to get dusty, only take it down once I was in too deep!

We Christians tend to get real spiritual as a means of not having to make the hard decisions and do the hard work. <u>We just "kiss it up to God" and keep going. This isn't faith; this is witchcraft!</u> Wow, I hadn't thought of it this way, but yes – witchcraft! <u>And how disappointed God must be, to have his children in the house of the Lord, giving power to such, but with</u>

praises to God!  We hide under our religion for protection from the hard stuff!  We think that if we do "A", "B" and "C", He will keep "X", "Y" and "Z" from happening to us!  We barter with God, which isn't the same as trusting in God.

Another parameter of this earthly realm is "time".  We know that, given time, we can figure things out, resolve things, learn things, fix things, etc.  People use time as commerce more than we use money.  However, if when we put on our "spiritual hats", we remove our "earth-realm hats", then we feel that we can ignore the usefulness of time, because we perceive that we are being "spirit led" – and "in God, there is no time."  So, we make some decisions that otherwise should have waited, and we expect God to fix the resultant consequences – "God Dust".

Case in point: Many Christians get engaged and married quite quickly, siting reasons such as, "If God put it together, who are we to insist that we have to wait to see if it's right."  Or, "God brought us together, so He will make it work," or, "We did it right (meaning we abstained), so God will bless our union."  Or, we use the scripture, "Better to marry than to burn!"  That's because if you're abstaining, the biggest unspoken sentiment is that you don't want to have to abstain from sex much longer.  Or, if you're not abstaining, you get married quickly so as not to "live in sin" any longer.

I was guilty of most of the above sentiments for both marriages.  I have come to realize that the healthiest way to look at it is that we should apply the common-sense parameters while praying for guidance and awaiting His answers.  We should not even talk about marrying someone whom we haven't spent enough time getting to know.  In a year, you will know a lot, but probably not nearly enough.  But if you're already planning to marry, the other can keep up the pretense knowing there's only a short while to do so.  So the advantage to dating for longer is that if there isn't a marriage on the horizon, then he might exhaust himself with the charades and slip up, showing his true character and intent!

Now this is the point where I will get many dissenters.  Many will say that it doesn't take a lot of time; that they or people they know have lived happily married for decades, having dated only a short time.  True!  But listen to what is inferred.  If there is something to come out, like charades/games being played, then time tells.  Now, if there never were charades in the relationship, then one day is all it takes! So, time reveals things if there are things to reveal. And many people have gigantic things that need to be revealed. Now, everyone has flaws, so I am not talking about flaws. I'm talking about charades of secret agendas, fraudulence or deceitful behavior. Or it could be that the problem isn't malice, but there could just be a truly challenging "issue" that needs to be uncovered and worked on with intervention.

*This weekend, my brother voiced about the healthiest idea about marriage I've ever heard. He is the brother who never wed, so decade after decade I'd ask him if he was seeing anyone or even interested in marrying. On the heels of our conversation about how my marriage should have never happened, he said that he has NO desire to get married, unless he meets the right one. He didn't say he wants to get married and hopes to find the right one. Nor did he say he only wants to get married IF he meets the right one. He said he has NO desire to get married UNLESS he finds the right one!*

*This is the opposite of what I've said all my life! I've always said, "I want to get married!" Then, I put God to the task of sending someone who fits the bill. But God knows every one's volitional mind, and so He knows what will happen. So I believe that He protects us from many prospects; I also believe that some of us are so persistent that He'll relent, even though that person we think fits the bill really isn't best for us.*

*My brother also said that he would not even think about marrying someone whom he hasn't verified as a Christian and right for him, and that it can take years for that to happen. My brother is one of the strongest Christians I know, and he* isn't spiritualizing the process and shortening it by "playing the God card", which is: "God will make it work!"

If God put it together, then find out if He did by giving it time! What if God gave him to us, but we moved ahead of God's timing? Again, if no one is playing games and there are no secret agendas, then a quick courtship and marriage can yield a lifetime of bliss. But we don't know. So why risk jumping into a marriage where there may be huge "issues" that can derail even the happiest of beginnings? And even these can be worked out during the marriage if there is true love and willingness on both sides. But not where there is fraud and deceit, as in my case.

### ENJOYING MY NEW DIRECTION!

*Saturday, October 25$^{th}$, 2014*

*Stanton took me to see "The Trip to Bountiful", with the fabulous Cicely Tyson, Vanessa L. Williams and Blair Underwood. We had great seats... near the front. Stanton also treated me to lunch at the Elephant Bar and dinner in Hollywood at Roscoe's. Great time! Great man! I am so blessed to have a wonderful man in my life like Stan!*

*Friday, October 31$^{st}$, 2014*

*On yesterday, I went to the SB County courthouse and filed my Proof of Service from Dick being served on 10/03. I also got next filing instructions from self-help and was out of there in about two hours. I checked back with Shanette, and she confirmed that she hadn't left yet for her timeshare that she had invited me to. I was so happy to be able to join her that afternoon.*

We had a nice drive through Newport Beach and down PCH. After we sat on the patio talking and watching the sun set, we grilled chicken and vegys, and I broke the news. She was expecting something, she said, since I had been trying to get with her. She said she also suspected something when I showed up at Kim's wedding without Dick. We talked about it for about three hours, and then we enjoyed our stay.

We Jacuzzied and played pool after this, and that night, I slept on the pull-out in the living room. I had the slide glass window to the patio open, and I enjoyed the beautiful half-moon descending right into the ocean. The sound of the ocean waves was music to my ears, and I fell asleep to it. We had a good breakfast, and then we went bike riding along the beach. That was a great get-away, and well needed! Thank you Father... and Shanette! I have noticed that in my times of financial hardship, God has provided great vacations and get-aways for me... free of charge! Thank you, God!


November 5th, 2014

On Monday, Nov 3rd, I verified that Dick had not yet filed. So on the 4th, I filed my Request to Enter Default by fax. Today, I met Shanette on the job for her to mail the change of hearing date notification to Dick and the proof of mailing to the court. I'm done with that process for a few days. I will, however, prepare my judgment and hearing docs in a few days.

After my business with Shanette, I dropped in on Jeremy [my son], and we talked for 2.5 hours. It was very productive and relaxing. He even agreed to come and take care of my pool the next day.

Thursday, November 6th, 2014

I'm in a good place. I love it! I love life! I am in-tune with the Holy Spirit, letting Him guide me. He has led me into quiet waters; He has restored my soul! He restored my peaceful home! No more of that spirit of deceit and dissention living here in this house! And just being in this place of retirement – being able to take it slowly and do what I want, when I want – is phenomenal! Not to have to trade my life for a paycheck is so freeing and empowering! I'm young and healthy and free! And God gives me witty ideas for future businesses! And meanwhile, even while recovering from the financial setback of marital debt, He is supplying me with enough income on which to live. I thank God!

I love that He has led me out of that marriage! I still wonder, however, why or if He led me in it. But did He lead me, or was I misled? I conclude that He didn't, and yes, I was misled. Regardless, my book is the result; this book is meant to be very, very useful to many women! The principle of Romans 8:28 is at work here: "And we know that God works all things together for the good of those who love Him, who are called according to His purpose." Yes, God took a mess and made it a message! So let me get back to it.

## Chapter 17: AN EPIPHANY!

*Friday, November 7th, 2014*

*When I was at Jeremy's place, I had an epiphany. I was observing him in his "not so great" apartment, wondering what steps he'd take at this point in his life to get himself to the next level... hopefully, returning to school and to a better job and apartment. Then in parallel, I saw Dick in his bachelor state, seeing his opportunity to get to the next level. I could imagine how Dick could see "getting his upgrade on" by marrying me and moving in with me. He saw a stable mature woman who had her own spacious home with enough bedrooms for all his kids, with amenities and who was driving a nice car. She cooked for him daily and even provided a few dollars. She could also serve as a "cover", not "lover", since he was struggling with his sexual dysfunction. So he set out to be this woman's "everything".*

### FAKE FRIEND FLASHBACK

*He was so nice and attentive when we dated. In fact, I remember his attentiveness being so overwhelming, that it seemed to be artificial. Now that should have been a clue to me! There were two things he did that annoyed and confused me. Now, I loved it when he constantly stroked me when we sat together, but he would keep doing that when we ate together on the couch or at the table. I remember thinking that this was so weird and bothersome. I wanted to be able to eat without the constant stroking, because it just felt weird while eating. Now I know why it felt weird! Because it was artificial; it was concocted and contrived! It was part of his deceptive behavior designed to win me over.*

*The other action was more apparent as artificial, yet I didn't understand what it meant at the time. He used to act like he was catching me from behind, as though I was falling, but I wasn't! He'd chuckle and say, "I don't want you to fall and hurt yourself!" It was so weird, but he thought he was ingratiating himself; showing himself to be a protector. But there was no present threat. He did it a lot, and it was so contrived. But I didn't know the genesis of it, so I didn't make anything of it. I didn't know to connect the dots! And the other weird thing about it was that there was a time that I actually was falling and he did nothing, even though he was nearby.*

In retrospect, I realize that he had to manufacture "manly" behavior to compensate for his lack of inherent manliness. And another epiphany I just had was that his artificial "catches" were manufactured to ingratiate himself! I realize that we all put our best foot forward when dating, but to manufacture something to twist another's beliefs about you is a far stretch. It is deceit! And now, connecting the dots, I see that it was one of his actions just to show off the action, but not to be useful. Like his dishwashing. I noticed when we were dating and beyond, that his dish washing was atrocious! It seemed that he just dipped the dishes in soapy water and rinsed, because pots and other dishes still had food on them afterward! It occurred to me that he just washes dishes to say that he washed the dishes, not to get them clean. There is a big difference! And that is how he approached his actions; they were artificially induced to solicit a reaction of trust and appreciation. But he had to do this, because he was insincere. A sincere person does not have to set up scenarios to ingratiate himself and make people trust and appreciate him.

# PHASE 4 – PARADIGM SHIFT!

## Chapter 18: "COURT'S IN SESSION!"

Saturday, November 22$^{nd}$, 2014

I have finally recovered from the whirlwind of the last few days. This was supposed to be my victory lap! In fact, I had called a friend ahead of time to make arrangements to have a victory celebration for the night of my hearing. I was just that confident that I would win my money back at the hearing, because, after all, Dick clearly owed me the money! Well, the judicial system is a horse of a different color! "Justice" is not necessarily the goal! So here's what happened.

I went into court on Wednesday, November 19, at 8:30 am. Dick shows up late, but they let him in anyway. My case is finally called about two hours later. The commissioner calls us up, and we approach the bench and are seated. I wait for her to tell me that I can speak, but she doesn't. Then it comes: She says, "So I see that you're asking for attorney's fees, but I see that you're self-represented; so are you looking to get some money just in case one day you might decide to get an attorney?" Whoa! She came straight out of the gate with bias, sarcasm, and accusation! I asked, "May I please address that?" She said, "No!" Then she moved on to the next subject. She said, "I see you're asking for alimony, but you've only been married for nine months, and you've been separated for half that time, and usually, alimony is considered in cases of long-term marriages of ten years or more. You still have the money you came into the marriage with," reading my income source; then she carried on some more. I again asked her if I may speak, and she again said, "No!" When she finally did allow me to speak, I said I am here for my default judgment of the debt repayment. She interrupted me and said "No you're not! You are here for alimony and attorney's fees!" I tried to respond that "I had checked the box for temporary spousal support for the repayment of the debt he owes," but she again interrupted and said, "That is a debt matter! This hearing is not for debt, but for alimony and attorney's fees!" Then I said, "Going back to your first point about attorney's fees, I did not indicate that I wanted attorney's fees. I checked the box for 'Or Costs'. I listed my filing costs that I'd like reimbursed." She tried to act like my request for $650 was ridiculously high for just filing fees, so I reiterated that the costs are itemized. She said, "Well, the filing fee is only $200!" Again, I referred her to the itemization and stated that "The filing fee is $425, and the hearing fee is $60, and the Turbo Court filing fee is...," then she interrupted me again and retorted, "The Turbo Court fee is just a convenience fee for not having to stand in line!" Then she stopped me from reading off the other costs associated with my filing and ended it with a judgment that the respondent repay only $515 of the $650 costs, and she gave him an entire two months in which to repay it! Then I tried to ask her when she would hear about the debt, but she wouldn't let me speak, and she said she would not advise me, saying, "I am not your lawyer!" She said she suggests that I go to the self-help resource center. So I did... immediately after she dismissed us.

These past three days... I've just been in a stupor! This man defrauded me before, during and after the marriage! He rolled up to the courthouse on tires that he had charged to _my_ card and wouldn't repay me for, and then walked out of there with favor! Unbelievable!

How could I be going through such mess and had done nothing wrong? All I did was marry the man I loved and thought loved me! And then I endured being married to a man who did not make love to me, no longer told me he loved me, stopped showing affection to me and wouldn't pay me attention or pay bills! Yet I had done so much for him! When we first started dating, he had no job; I fed him every day - two times a day - and when he did get a job, I fed him dinner every day. Plus, I forked out $6K before our marriage for expenses he was to have repaid. I carried him before and during the marriage; yet this commissioner tries to paint me as some woman marrying Dick just to get out of there in nine months with his money! I'm just speechless! Such a disservice was done to me!

It felt so much like I had entered into a realm of this earth that God's grace and mercy had not even penetrated! Not because of the outcome; I just felt something else at work in that courtroom - another influence! It is such a remarkably strange feeling of dissonance - when you've been used to walking in grace and mercy!

Oh, readers, if any of you don't know God the Father through the grace and mercy of Jesus Christ, I invite you to enter! Because, if in this instance, I felt what it's like to be in a realm seemingly devoid of His grace and mercy, then it must be hell to walk in it every day! Because for the unsaved, it doesn't take walking into a realm of un-Godly influence; if you're not a Christian, your entire world is subject to demonic control, because the grace of Jesus' redemption isn't covering you!

[I feel like I want to interject something here before you move on to my next point. At my church's youth-Sunday service in mid-May 2016, our youth pastor, Minister Monique, taught the lesson from Luke 10:18-19, which says, "I saw Satan fall like lightning from heaven. I have given you authority to trample on snakes and scorpions and to overcome all the power of the enemy; nothing will harm you." I'm interjecting this, because my journal entry below does not make it clear that we do have the "power"! In the first verse, Jesus, makes it plain that He was on the scene from the beginning, and that He saw Satan cast out (which infers that he is subject to one more powerful)! Then Jesus goes on to say that He has given us (Christians) authority over him! So, to clarify my entry above: no, Christians don't experience a realm devoid of God's grace, because we are covered by the blood of Christ and we've been given authority! So, we live in this world where Satan's dominion exists, but as Minister Monique said... "Who's runnin' this?!!!!"]

The enemy has control over this earth because it was given to him through the fall of man in Genesis 3. God still controls the universe, and hence still has authority over the earth, but when sin entered the earth, sin ushered in its author, Satan, as prince of the air (this earth). So it's like the devil is the COO of the earth, but he still has to answer to the CEO! Satan can operate freely in the earth realm, but he must answer to the chief executive officer – God! If you read the book of Revelation, you will see where Jesus takes back the title deed to the earth; but until then, Satan has dominion over the earth. But thank God for grace! Because of grace through His son, Jesus, those who receive Jesus are not under the control of Satan. Though we live in a world controlled by Satan, we ourselves are not controlled by Satan, once we receive Christ and yield to Him!

[Read Romans 5:12, 2 Corinthians 4:4, Ephesians 2:2, Ephesians 6:12, 1 John 5:19, Luke 4:5-7, Acts 26:18, Colossians 1:13–14, Romans 16:20, John 12:31 and Revelation 5:9]

So often, the only distinction referred to for Christians is our heavenly destination, as opposed to hell. Great distinction, I must say! But while we're on earth, the greatest distinction is – who is in control of me... God or Satan? Before receiving Christ, even if we're considered really good, Satan has great access if he chooses to control some aspect of us. Once on "Team Jesus", however, Satan must ask permission for access. Remember in "Job", where Satan was given permission by God to mess with Job? Well, without permission, he can't! That's good news! Enough of a reason to become a Christian!

Now, here's another distinction. Even as Christians, we may not yield ourselves to God and His will; thus, we're yielding access to Satan's influence. That's why, in Christian talk, we use the phrase, "walking with Christ". It is a constant yielding of your will to His – keeping us up under God's umbrella of protection from Satan's influence. But even while under there, for whatever reason, God can and sometimes does grant permission to the enemy to mess with us! And as any good COO would, Satan has "systems" in place to do his job: to ensnare all mankind.

This system to which I refer is called the "Seven Mountains System", and it is comprised of these areas: Government and Law; Education; Entertainment and Arts; Religion; Family; Business; and Media. The "Seven Mountains" term describes institutions that mankind has set up to enhance our world, which is fine. But within these, Satan has set up a systematic "sphere of influence", resulting in control (schemes). Hence, the enemy uses them to control whole groups of people to think the same way for ultimate dominion. But the story isn't over. When prayed up and through grace, we can still win the victory! It just takes a fight! This is why we are admonished to "Put on the full armor of God so that you can take your stand against the devil's schemes," (Ephesians 6:11).

Remember that the devil's mission is to "kill, steal and destroy" (John 10:10). So of course he has his ammunition! For instance, in the area of government and law, his most successful system may be corruption. In the area of arts and entertainment we see a domination of immorality. In education we see a systematic elimination of the "creation" ideology, etc. Yes, of course we all live, work and partake of all of these institutions, but we can and should resist the pull toward the systemic viewpoints and behaviors. This is usually done in connection with a relationship with God and His Word (the Bible). So applying the Word of God to all areas of life is a defense against the "Seven Mountains Dominion". The Word supplies direction and defense. It is offensive and it is defensive in our day to day encounters. [Apply it like therapy, as my friend and church member, Karen Foote describes in her book, "Word Therapy".]

Do your research on these areas called dominionism. Of course there's no scriptural reference to it in particular. It is a means of categorizing the major institutions through which Satan seems to have set up dominion. So do an online search, but here's a warning: be very careful about the context of some of the information sources. Ironically, one source that I read uses teaching on this area and then aligns their false teachings with it, to give their own agendas merit.

*I met with Pastor Ken two days after the hearing, and he confirmed what I had been thinking. He said that he knew of the influence of the Seven Mountains Dominion via the court system, and that's why he had us to fast and pray before my hearing. He was right! I know that when I stepped into that courtroom, I stepped into another world where the enemy has an unjust influence already in place so that when you enter it, you are "caught up!"*

*This is the term I used as I watched others there. They were just there to bring their bad marriages to a legal close and to work out child custody and support issues. Those who use this system are just trying to correct a wrong… to get some justice. But the justice system holds them captive; I saw them moving about like zombies under the court system's control. This is an injustice to people already hurting. Whether through corruption or abuse of power, justice is not always delivered.*

*I wish that the "justice" system were run more like a corporation, where we are treated as customers worthy of good customer service. I also wish that since the law makes it so difficult to navigate through a divorce, they would make it* as difficult to get married. Since they require mediation, time to lapse, hearing continuances, etc., why not require all of this prior to granting marriage licenses? Why not require a time period for pre-marital counseling instead of divorce mediation down the road? Yes, counseling is expensive, but divorce is hundreds to thousands of times more expensive! Better yet, why not require "Relationship 101" courses in high school? Since over 50% of married couples will end up divorced, why not try to change those stats where it counts? Not once the problems start, but before the marriage starts!

Well anyway, all those prayers for me did not go to waste! No; prayers CAN and DO penetrate even the Seven Mountains Dominion! They are no match for God! I did not lose my case. I was just smeared through the mud; that's all. It just felt badly, but I did not lose. I'm just experiencing a delay. Remember, Jacob wrestled with an angel and was told that his prayer had been answered 21 days ago. But his prayer was hindered by the Prince of Persia, so God had to send a prince to deal with a prince! He sent Archangel Michael to fight and subdue the Prince of Persia! Well, God did send in bigger forces to fight this system, and I'm in that period of delay right now; but I won't stay there!

"UPHILL JOURNEY"

Saturday, November 29th, 2014

On Thursday, Thanksgiving, I went to [my cousins] Ethel and Brenda's home in Inglewood. My kids went to their dad's.

Over dinner, I shared with the two about the whole marital situation. I was there for five hours having a great time. On Friday, [my friend] Regena invited me to use her extra ticket to go to Culver City for Gentleman G's Black Friday Steppers' Ball with her boyfriend and visiting daughter. Tonight, we are all going to Flapper's Comedy Club, where my daughter is manager.

Sunday, November 30th, 2014

In church today, for the first time, a few people did directly ask me about "my husband". I was ready to talk about it, so I did. It's something how, when I was ready to talk about it, people started asking. Before, they were very general and just asked "How's Dick?" I would say with a smile, "Great!" And he was great, because he had gotten away with fraud for the meanwhile – driving on four new free tires and having gone to Puerto Rico earlier this year, free! He's all good – for now! And Friday at the steppers' ball, two people asked, and I was fine with telling them. In fact, one of them told me that he was surprised that I was even with Dick. He said that when he first saw us together, he had thought to himself that I could do much better... that it looked like I was settling! Now I know that he was right!

The message today in church was again, really good. Pastor Ken spoke of "waiting just a little while," from 1 Peter 5:10. "And the God of all grace, who called you to his eternal glory in Christ, after you have suffered a little while, will himself *restore you and make you strong, firm and steadfast." So using this analogy, the valley comes before the mountain-top experience. Even if you've already made it to the base of the mountain, it is a difficult journey to the top; so comparatively, you're in a valley! And even if you find a winding road to take you more easily to the top, it winds you round about in an indirect fashion.*

I really appreciate Pastor Ken's sermons because they are cinematic; he paints a picture with his words, and so I see his teachings as visions that I remember. I could envision a person walking along on a bright sunny day, on flat land with beautiful surroundings, enjoying the journey on the way to the mountain. Then, out of nowhere, the terrain drops, either suddenly or gradually, to a valley. Then the scenery turns to a dark ugly, dry environment. However, this is where the enemy gets a lot of us. This appears to be a delay, which makes us want to stop the journey. This delay makes us think of it as a blockage or that we're on the wrong path, instead of a momentary derailing. So we think we are to stop, question our journey, or even turn back for what were greener pastures in our past.

Or we think we're waiting for circumstances to change before we continue our journey, so we stop and hide-out. We literally wait by staying in one place instead of moving. But that would be just a holding pattern, not progress. I recall another message of Pastor Ken's, where he dispelled what we think of as "waiting on the Lord." Instead of thinking of the definition of pausing or stopping, think of a waitress "waiting" on her customers. She is not pausing; she is actively serving and working towards an end!

Therefore, we should be in a progression towards the desired outcome. The mountain is still in view, so just keep on walking towards it; you will get out of the valley and reach that mountain, and then that peak! So it's all good! Just keep on walking. We use the term, "walking in faith", and that pretty much symbolizes walking, pursuing, pressing on and progressing while praying. And in God's timing, it comes to pass. But if we stop pressing on and we only pray, it makes our prayers look futile when nothing comes to pass. In fact, it makes the enemy look victorious and us hopeless.

This is just a time lapse for our efforts to pay off. It is likened to the principle of seedtime and harvest. There is a time lapse between our efforts of planting the seed and the harvest. As Pastor Ken said, "We don't go pull up the seeds just because we haven't seen anything spring up! We keep watering them... and pulling the weeds." We plant our seeds of prayer, and we water with praise and worship and serving, and we weed with discernment along the way.

It is called the journey. We accept that time is built into the process of seedtime and harvest, and it would really help if we realized that time is built into the human process of reaching our destinations. When we're driving from point "A" to point "B", we are on our journey. The same for our life's destinations. But we have to keep pressing forward to that destination with prayer and the Holy Spirit's leading as our vehicle.

So instead of thinking of it in terms of delay, derailment or an impasse, how about just seeing it as part of our journey to get to the other side or to get up that mountain. A journey is dynamic, not static! We won't get to the other side if we're static! We must press ahead! Any valleys and twists and turns and ugly landscaping are part of the journey. It was already there along the way. It's not coming for you. We just got on the road towards a destination, and adversity was on the path! (And remember, Satan is the prince of this earth!) The valley and bad environment are already part of the terrain, but if we desire the mountain-top experience, we must move through the existing terrain. And sometimes the existing terrain can even be comfortable, so we hang out in the land of complacency. We spiritualize it by calling it "God's blessings". And maybe it is... for a season. But don't stay there too long. We wouldn't appreciate the mountain-top were it not for valleys we've experienced. And we wouldn't be strengthened except for resistance.

We learn things along the way, and we are strengthened by the journey. Remember the story of the chicks trying to hatch from their shells? The breaking-out experience is actually a strengthening process for their wings. Once hatched after the experience of resistance, their wings are strengthened for flight! And if some kind animal-loving person decides to circumvent that seemingly difficult experience for the chicks by removing the shells for them, they are born with no strength in their wings, and they won't be able to fly! How tragic! God knows what we need in our lives for strength!

And as Pastor Ken said today, it is a faith-walk; not a hope-walk. We're not hoping we'll get to the mountain-top. We have faith that we will, because we are applying the action of walking to the belief that God has done His part. Faith is action. We must walk! It is not enough that we see the mountain in the distance; we must walk to it, trusting that God will show us the best path.

[I'd like to add another element here to this faith-walk. It is profession... or a confession of what you're believing to happen. A few years ago (in the very best sermon I've ever heard in my entire life), Pastor Ken taught that "Confession is to faith, what thrust is to lift!" An airplane needs thrust to lift; as well, we need to speak/confess what we have faith to happen. I urge you to go to Point of Grace's web site and order that dynamic CD!]

With respect to my own circumstances, my journey is taking some twists and turns; I have some detours, but I am no longer derailed. My victory will take a few more steps than I had anticipated. Just because I'm in the right, doesn't mean my journey will be quick and without hardship. I see the mountain-top, and I will keep on walking the path before me. God told Moses to tell Pharaoh, "Let my people go!" Just because God initiated this, doesn't mean it would be instantaneous! God even hardened Pharaoh's heart, so it took ten times for Moses! This could have been over several weeks or months! But it was going to happen, because God appointed it to; so we have that confidence!

## Chapter 19: FORGIVENESS

*Tuesday, December 2$^{nd}$, 2014*

*On yesterday, I was on my 1$^{st}$ day of my morning fast, because on Sunday, Minister Cherry from church had prayed with me, and she prayed specifically that God would put a fasting spirit on me. I had not thought of fasting, but God certainly moved, because I declared a fast of five mornings for* the week. And during my fast I'm making it a point to pray in agreement with different sisters in the Lord.

God was moving through different sisters, because, on Monday night, Jheri and I walked in to Rev. class together from the parking lot, and I thought that I'd like to open up to her and share about my marital situation. We ended up in the bathroom together, so I took the opportunity to share. Jheri was so supportive and loving. At some point, we were interrupted, so we resumed our conversation via phone today during her lunch hour. That is when she prayed a prayer that God used to change my thinking. I noticed that her prayers were about God convicting Dick's heart, softening Dick's heart, and reaching Dick to break up the fallow ground. I was thinking that this was a very gentle approach to the hard approach of avoidance that he's used with me. And gentle compared to my past prayers of, "God, rebuke Dick!" Then, she stated that I was going to have to work on forgiveness. I thought this was just something generic that a person would pray, and that I didn't have a problem with unforgiveness. I really felt that since I wasn't consumed with anger, that I didn't have unforgiveness in my heart.

During my prayer with Jheri, I keyed in on her prayer that God convict Dick to do the right thing; also on her characterizing his behavior as betrayal and my need to forgive him. It occurred to me that I need to give him a chance to redeem himself. Yes, he is wrong and I am right, but that doesn't mean he can't repent and pay his debt. If he is a Christian, that is entirely possible, especially with prayer. For his own sake, I should give him a chance. Now, I had already decided it would be good to seek mediation about his debt, but I hadn't looked at it as mediation for his sake – to allow him to make the decision to pay me – hence to repent. That would be the ultimate act of forgiveness. I can keep praying for a judgment against him and get it, but that's only good for me; it doesn't redeem my brother. But to bring it to him as an opportunity to do right is good for us both.

This is derived from scripture that says that a husband's prayers are hindered when he has wronged his wife. 1 Peter 3:7 states, "Husbands, in the same way be considerate as you live with your wives, and treat them with respect as the weaker partner and as heirs with you of the gracious gift of life, so that nothing will hinder your prayers." Likewise, God says don't even bring your gifts to the altar, if you have aught against your brother, Matthew 5: 23, 24. "Therefore if you are presenting your offering at the altar and there remember that your brother has something against you, leave your offering there before the altar and go; first be reconciled to your brother, and then come and present your offering." Drilling this down even further, God even said that a man who doesn't take care of his own household is worse than an infidel (unbeliever), 1 Timothy 5:8. "But if any provide not for his own, and especially for those of his own house, he hath denied the faith, and is worse than an infidel."

Dick is guilty of all of this, and as a believer, I should be willing to help restore him. Once the judgment is made, he has no opportunity to initiate redemption. And nothing will go right for him if he does not do right by his wife and by God, according to God's word. [No, this was not Miss Celie's quote from "The Color Purple"! LOL! This is straight from the word of God!] So, I will reach out to him for mediation; for him, not for me.

*But I know how he gets when there is an important topic on the table, so in using wisdom, I want a third party to mediate. I feel he'd be more receptive to this third party initiating the mediation also. I had already asked Dr. Z. to mediate the week of the hearing, and he is willing, but he is not willing to call and ask him to; and of course Dick avoids me. I will be praying with others for direction on this; about the right person to approach about mediating... or that God just arranges it.*

As a side note, Dick came to Rev. class last night, but didn't come in when he saw me! What kind of games is he playing? I've tried to get in his head, to imagine how he could live with himself; all I could come up with is that he is so used to being a user! In his self-centered way, he probably excuses his actions and perhaps even plays the victim. Maybe he is over there thinking I'm wrong for divorcing him, and thus he is absolved of his debt! And I already know that he thought he shouldn't have had to split household expenses with me when we were married, as he told the therapist. So he resented spending money on the household and me then, so of course he resents it now. What an infidel! Yes, many people who've heard my story believe he's not really a believer, as the word "infidel" implies. Well, let's give him a chance to repent.

Tuesday, December 9th, 2014

Wow! God is good! He always was, and is, and is to come! It's just great to have specific testimonies that come as a result of specific prayer and fasting. God used Jheri's compassionate prayer and her comments to work on me the rest of the week. So to my surprise, this is how I've been praying for the week! God showed me that I did need to be even more forgiving. I realized that my attitude towards Dick should be in accordance with Matt 5:23-24 and Mark 11:25, meaning that I should want to see my brother restored to God and to me.

The Matthew scripture speaks to the offender, saying to reconcile with your brother before you give your offerings. Thus, I should want this for him for his sake, not for mine, so that God would accept his offerings; and Dick would be blessed accordingly. But Mark 11:25, 26 says that I need to forgive the offender, lest I not be forgiven. "And when ye stand praying, forgive, if ye have aught against any; that your Father also which is in heaven may forgive you your trespasses. But if ye do not forgive, neither will your Father which is in heaven forgive your trespasses." So this one is for me.

If I were truly forgiving, I wouldn't use terms of retribution in prayer to God to deal with him. Instead, I'd be more interested in God's conviction of his heart than his punishment. Jeremy even concurred, when he was over last week and I was sharing with him about my new attitude. He said, that maybe, in Dick's own retarded way, he really believes he is in the right, and he is not over there feeling badly about how he has treated me; thus he is not repenting for anything. Then he needs to be convicted by God of his wrong. And Jeremy said that therefore, he needs to stop referring to Dick as a "dick!"

Thus, we both need to sit down and talk for reconciliation. And the offender needs restoration to God. This is foremost. Reconciliation to God should result in making amends to the one offended; this is secondary. So the restoration of my funds will be an outpouring of his reconciliation with God and with me.

## CALLUSES OF THE HEART

What if, in addition to feeling that he's right, his heart has been hardened?  So we were right for praying that God soften Dick's heart. And this hardness took place a long time ago. It isn't the result of the separation. I saw it back in February for the first time when we had an argument; I saw hatred in his eyes that surprised me. And when I saw him at Rev. class in September and then at court in November, I saw a stone cold look on his face. Now I know that his countenance reflected a stone hard-heart! I thought he just hated me, and I couldn't figure out why. But it was a hardness of heart that was reflected in his eyes and on his face! This by itself is a revelation! And the good news is that we can pray that God soften hearts!

But I'm sure that this hardness took place even in the aftermath of his last divorce, and of course during the hard parts of that marriage. My friend told me about the very public divorce. And he also confirmed one of my suspicions, which was that his reactions towards me were simply reactions to his former wife. So scales had formed even years before we were together. I'm recalling that his mom told him that he shouldn't get married again...

Over time and as issues compound, scales form, callouses build, and the enemy sets up strongholds. The enemy uses ego and pride and selfishness as evil spirits. He uses the spirit of entitlement and a deceiving spirit also. All of these factors build up to a hard and resistant heart, one of the enemy's finest tools! But some things are broken only through prayer and fasting. I've taken for granted how gracious God is in answering prayer over the years, with no fasting involved. Gotta be careful of that! If God's blessings make us conditioned to getting them without the full power of God working, then we're less inclined to exercise God's full power and thus get the best results. We need to exercise His full anointing power. If God says that there are some things He won't move on except for when we fast, then believe Him! Let's put on a fasting spirit!

## THOUGHT YOU OUGHT TO ADDRESS THE "AUGHT"!

*Tuesday, December 9th, 2014 (cont'd)*

*So, I had extended my 5-day breakfast fast to pray for the softening of Dick's heart. Then last night, I went to Rev. class, and there sat Dick! He had a softness about his countenance! I prayed during class to confirm if I were to approach him afterwards. I prayed specifically about the very words I'd use. God gave them to me. After class, I waited for him to finish talking to Jheri, whom he had greeted. After a while, I realized that instead of waiting to see him alone, God had already set it up for me to talk to Dick with* the very person who started this move of God... and who should be the counselor!

So I went up to them and greeted both, then I said: "Since you both are standing here together, I just want to say that, Dick, God has been dealing with me for a week now, ever since Jheri prayed with me last Monday. He's been dealing with me about the way you and I have been relating. Specifically, He has used two scriptures." Then I recited the two aforementioned scriptures. I said, "I would like to offer up an opportunity for us to meet and make amends." I kept looking into his face to read his countenance, which was, still soft! It reminded me of the old Dick... the one I knew before we were married.

He said, "Yes"! Wow! God did it! Wow! Praise the Lord! Yes! Hallelujah! He both softened Dick's heart, to where I saw it and heard it! Hallelujah! So we set the meeting date for Tuesday, Dec. 16$^{th}$ at 7 pm at her office! Yea! And she's actually a certified marriage and family therapist with a PhD and her own office! Hallelujah! And thinking back through the week, God had her in the parking lot with me, in the ladies' room with me, available to pray with me during my fast and during her lunch break, and then standing there next to him after God had softened his heart! God had a plan, and that plan definitely included Jheri!!!!! Thank God, and thank Jheri!

I feel so good about the prospect of reconciliation, and now I realize how far I've missed the mark. It has been half a year since our separation, and at that time, the idea was to work on us or to have an amicable dissolution. It was never to part as enemies. And I let his response to me a few weeks after our separation set the tone for him and for me. And I let the look that I deemed as "hatred" on his countenance push me away completely, instead of trying to reason with him. That "look" was a reflection of his hard heart, not a resolve that he hated me. This is a good time to state that <u>the enemy uses/creates hard hearts to do just that... discourage the other from doing the right thing. It is one of his best marriage busting tools!</u> It puts up a wall to discourage entry and resolution. Resolution doesn't necessarily mean getting back together. Wisdom has to enter. But in my case, it does mean that we can be amicable, and that if there is aught, then the offender ought to make amends.

*Since I'm in this new frame of thought – and frankly, a frame of freedom brought on only by forgiveness – I'm open, and hence I wondered if that means I'm open to the marriage. Before I went to bed last night, I pondered that, but quickly answered it in the negative. I know that it wasn't a marriage. Only God and I know that we were married without having a marriage! So no; we can be friends only – I'm open to that. I think this is why I had a crazy dream last night. I asked the Lord about its significance, and I believe His answer was this. In the dream, there was Val and Gary Ewing, the star-crossed lovers of [old TV series] "Knotts Landing". They were so in love, but people and things got in the way of their marriage and they divorced. They later became friends, but married and divorced others. In my dream, I was observing Gary in a cave filled with stacks of sheet-rock stacked to the top, and he was standing on them. He was on the phone with Val, and she had the choice to get back together with him; but she turned it down. I left the cave, because the setting was so dry and uninviting, and then the dream was over. I wondered why the setting, and why them. I believe my answer was that, even Val knew not to go back to Gary, and I know how "Gary-crazy" Val was. She knew there was nothing there. Well I know there's nothing in a marriage with Dick. It is very dry and uninviting. No love life... no sex life; I might as well had been living in that cave in my dream!*

FASTING FAST TRACKS YOUR PRAYERS!

*Wednesday, December 10$^{th}$, 2014*

This morning, I completed my 3$^{rd}$ morning of fasting this week, with two more to go. Last week's and this week's morning fasts have been so awesome; a phrase you normally would not associate with periods of starvation! But our awesome God knew how awesome a time a Christian can have in the Lord through a fast. It isn't punishment; it is an opportunity! The opportunity is to be more in-tune with God and more appreciative of the very one who keeps us alive via food, but whom we take so much for granted (food too). Every time a hunger pain strikes, ordinarily, we're already on our way to our kitchen to fulfil that need. But when fasting, we remember that we can't, and then we remember that it is by God's grace that we ordinarily can. And we remember why we're fasting; thus we remember to pray fervently – just as fervently as we are... hungry! And we want to squeeze out the most results we can out of our fast, so we call up sisters and brothers in the Lord to agree in prayer with us, as the Bible says. I know that I usually don't make a concerted effort to call different people daily to pray with, but since my fast is limited to a certain number of mornings, I plan on calling folks that number of days.

And the other awesome thing that fasting does is that once the fast is over, we are far more appreciative of the food God supplies us. We know that we can no longer take being able to eat for granted. Each afternoon that I have finally been able to put something in my mouth, I have been sooooo appreciative! I plan to fast more often from now on. And I do like the breakfast fasts more than other types, because I really am so appreciative when I get to eat, in the same day that I was so in-tune with

God. To have those two feelings toward God compounded in the same day gives an exponential sense of closeness to God. And the purpose is not to starve one's self and to be light-headed, crazy and angry. It is to be spiritually minded. So if a sickly or agitated feeling is replacing the spiritual sense, then you've defeated the purpose. Now, if you're not a breakfast eater or you wake up at the crack of noon, then breakfast fasting is not a fair choice for you – you'd be short-changing yourself and God.

But of course, the most awesome thing about fasting is the answered prayers! God says that some things come only through prayer and fasting. Since I don't know which things come only by prayer and fasting, I'd rather be on the offensive and declare a fast, just to be sure; just in case my issue fits into that category of needing fasting.

## WHAT DOES IT PROFIT A MAN...?

*Thursday, December 11th, 2014*

*I've thought about some of the things I'll say to Dick when we meet Tuesday. I don't think I want to say that I want to be friends, because that might mean something different to him than it means to me. I don't see us hanging out. I think we're past that. I don't want to state that my main concern is his health, because I don't want to offer to be his mother either. And I don't want to be his caretaker. That's probably what I would have become had I stayed with him! So God steered me from that! I believe what I'll say is that I forgive him, and that I will continue to do the only thing I really could when we were together, which is to be a sister in the Lord – regularly lifting him up in prayer. And he needs to make amends with me so that his prayers and offerings won't be hindered.*

*I am thinking of several more verses in addition to those previously cited: Mark 8:36, "For what does it profit a man to gain the whole world, and forfeit his soul?" The questions that Dick should really answer are: "Is not repaying your debt worth sacrificing a right relationship with God? Is gaining from me several thousand dollars' worth of worldly stuff worth losing your right standing with God? Is it worth God not answering your prayers? Is it worth not having a dime of your tithes and offerings being accepted by God?"*

*I'd want Dick reminded that, not only are your tithes and offerings for naught, but your communion-taking condemns you! God says to examine one's self before taking communion in 1 Corinthians 11:27-29. "Therefore whoever eats the bread or drinks the cup of the Lord in an unworthy manner, shall be guilty of the body and the blood of the Lord. But a man must examine himself, and in so doing he is to eat of the bread and drink of the cup. For he who eats and drinks, eats and drinks judgment to himself if he does not judge the body rightly..."*

*But during our mediation next week I probably wouldn't say all that. Instead, these are my sentiments:*

*It was never supposed to be this way. Our separation was supposed to be amicable. We were never supposed to be not speaking and at odds. In fact, we were amicable in the beginning, the weeks right after you moved. We were doing better in our relating than we had done in months of marriage. We would talk and text and see each other at Rev. class. It wasn't until the end of July, when I requested that* you mail a payment on the credit card balance (that I had already reminded you of before you left) that you responded no, and then you cut off communication. You stopped taking my calls and they would go straight to voicemail, and you stopped responding to my texts and voicemails. I realized that you had cut me off. I remember leaving you a voicemail asking "What is going on over there? Why won't you respond to my messages?" You never answered me.

I thought that I'd just give you some time, but at the same time, I was asking myself, "Time for what?" We were on good terms when you left. In fact, we were on better terms than before we had decided to separate. So what caused you to change on me? It was only when I had asked you to mail me a payment on the balance, since the bill was due, that you cut me off. Though you weren't speaking, this spoke volumes to me. It told me that there was a much bigger issue here – a character issue. You're cutting me off because I asked you for another payment on the credit card debt. The idea that you were sticking me with thousands of dollars of credit card debt was too much for me to process. I was in disbelief that you could do this to me and decided to believe otherwise. Since your response in July had been "No," because you had spent all your money on your kids' schools that month, I decided to believe that you would resume your payments the following month. It was far easier for me to believe that than to believe that you would betray me. So I waited an entire month.

Of course, I saw that you weren't coming to Rev. class, that you had avoided our friends' wedding that month, and that you never resumed conversation with me. But still I waited, to no avail. Back then, I had started talking with a close friend about what was going on, and she told me that Dick was not planning on paying that debt. I told her she was wrong, after all, she did not know him, and I did. He is a man of integrity and honor, I told her, and he just needed another month before resuming his payments. She told me Dick has me fooled. I actually got mad at her that she'd make such a statement about you, because I still believed in you. But it turns out she's right! Several more months have passed, and you haven't paid a dime on that debt.

I considered the fact that I might just need to go on and file for divorce. But then you showed up for class in mid-September; so I asked you if you'd please meet with Dr. Z. and me. You reluctantly said yes, and then you canceled the next day. That was the day that I realized that you were totally unwilling to talk and that we were through, so I started the divorce process that day.

I am still in amazement that it is even possible that you would stick me with a bill like that and cut off all communication with me. But my amazement is because I had thought of you in the category of people I know who are honorable and full of integrity. So I can hardly digest what is happening here.

# HIS "M.O."

*Tuesday, December 16th, 2014*

Well, this was the day that Dick was supposed to have redeemed himself to God through reconciliation with the sister he offended, via our mediation appointment. But of course, that didn't take place! Even though God had previously softened his heart and made way for the perfect mediator of that process, he stepped out of God's will and blocked it. Dick used his typical excuse to forego his responsibility to himself, God, Jheri and me. He texted me around noon today, stating that something came up with Jill and to tell Jheri he'd have to do it another time. I just couldn't believe it, yet I should have anticipated this. He has always used his kids as his excuse, and this is the fifth time he has canceled a counseling session. There was one right after our decision to separate; there were two right after we separated, there was one in September with Dr. Z., and then this one with Jheri! It is his M.O.; to avoid responsibility and accountability.

So, even though God worked a miracle in his heart by softening it, and even though my sisters and I agreed in prayer for another week that his heart be softened, Dick chose hardness of heart over God! His heart needs to be broken of the ego, pride, callouses, selfishness, strongholds, etc., that built up to the point of hardness of heart. These strongholds dictated his actions, even though there was temporary softening of his heart through prayer. <u>His old ways are in conflict with right decisions</u>. He has a habit of bailing; so he went with that. He is still self-centered, self-absorbed, selfish, childish, and unaccountable. This is just an accurate assessment; I'm not angry and taking it out on paper. Continued prayer about softness of heart just made him more approachable, but he was not really amenable. That's because he doesn't want to be accessible for accountability. But what he didn't realize is that this mediation was his opportunity to do exactly what the referenced scriptures stated to do. Accordingly, he would have restored himself to God's grace.

## A LEARNING EXPERIENCE!

Prayer works, but man can still exercise his free will and oppose God. So sometimes its work takes a long time, especially where there are strongholds. And the other side of that equation is whether or not the person you're praying for yields their strongholds for God to chisel at.

I am grateful for this learning opportunity about steadfast prayer. I see how important it is and how it really does move the hand of God in miraculous ways. This experience has made me a prayer warrior. I plan to regularly go to war about my kids, others and circumstances. I do not plan to let another "situation" drag me to having to fast. I plan to be proactive and declare fasts before situations get worse and before my loved ones go through!

*Another learning experience came as a result of my prayer partners. I had several of them, and I learned some valuable lessons about with whom to have to prayer of agreement. Not everyone should be selected. They all mean well, but we all come from different teachings. Intercessory prayer and prayer of agreement are two different prayers. And neither is a time to try to impose one's opinion, but to pray for God's answer. I had one sister slip in a prayer that Dick and I stay together! That might be her desire, but it is not mine, thus it does not belong in a prayer of agreement! And she knew I didn't agree with this, because I had shared with her why it wasn't and couldn't be a marriage. But when we prayed, she imposed her "pray and stay" opinion anyway. She should have just said, we're not in agreement, thus we cannot agree in prayer.*

I'm praying about reconciliation and restoration of a friendship and brother and sister relationship; not of our marriage. Again, it never was a marriage, and it is unconsummatable. We'd just be roommates, so why go back to that; that is not a marriage. Another sister snuck something similar in. She prayed that not only would there be a friendship rekindled, but love and affection and romance and restoration of intimacy! I was cringing by that point and shaking my head! "No!" I said. "I don't agree to this!" And did she forget that there wasn't intimacy; so how can it be rekindled?

Matthew 18:19 says, "If two people agree in prayer…" The two must be in agreement first. It isn't up for debate. It is not a forum for discussion. That should be done before the prayer, and if there are points of disagreement, those should be omitted from the prayer. Do not slip something in that wasn't agreed upon. Respect the party who asked you to agree in prayer with him or her.

## MO' OF HIS M.O.!

Wednesday, December 17th, 2014

Due to my latest prayers being more about softening of hearts, I believe mine became more vulnerable to the pain of the betrayal. In the beginning, I looked more at the fraud aspect, which was the result, but lately I've been experiencing the weight of the reality of his betrayal, which was the culprit! So my anger turned to hurt. This betrayal hurt my heart! Although this pain of betrayal had been settling in *lately, I did wake up this morning with a smile on my face. God's got this!*

*As I lay in bed, I thought a lot about Dick's crisis, and now I pray that I recall it all to write it down. Dick has a history of avoidance behavior, the manifestations of which tie him into a crisis state. He is in a relational, spiritual and health crisis. His ways have culminated in a state of crisis, and I'll explain each area.*

*I noticed one of his ways early on in the marriage, and that is passive-aggressive behavior. I would better characterize it as passive-avoidance behavior. He avoided any conversation that would hold him accountable to anything. Then he'd go on for days not speaking to me, just because I had the audacity to bring a subject up (usually bill paying). For the first four months of our marriage, he was only tipping me. He wouldn't pay anywhere near half of our household expenses. He blamed it on his pay raise not having come through yet. However, even at that point, had he paid his half, he still would have had $400 left over for himself! But he wouldn't. He gave me the $400 or less and would keep the rest.*

*I do recall one day, as I was washing dishes and he was sitting at the dinner table, that I finally brought up how it made me feel that he made me lose the safari trip deposit and never said he was sorry or that he would repay me for the loss. I also cited that it is costing the others on the trip much more money, due to our absence. He blurted out, "I don't care a bit about them!" I was appalled that the man I thought to be so honorable could have this sentiment. But at my bringing it up, he still didn't bother to apologize to me or promise repayment [only later in our only counseling session did he blurt out that he'd repay me]. He was still very much behind on catching up for those first four months. But for the first time, he admitted that he knew that he hadn't held up his end. I was very surprised about this admission, so I stopped there.*

I bring this up, because I was so used to his operating in his M.O. of "accessibility/accountability-avoidance", that I really thought that he didn't understand the concept of being responsible. I'm not being sarcastic. I had begun to see that he was more like a boy than a man by that time (about six months), and I had changed my expectations accordingly. I stopped expecting him to do what he should, when he should or because he should... which, by the way, defines an adult! I could only ask and remind, but not expect it automatically. So when he made that admission, it shocked me and made me realize that there had not only been lack of responsibility, but also lack of integrity as it relates to being fair to me.

In his avoidance behavior, he denied me access to him so that he could avoid accountability. This means he never meant to be responsible in the first place. If you're going to do right, then why would you run from someone asking if you're going to do right? He has some faulty thinking – some wires crossed. I see that he is still a little boy, and his childish ways have landed him in a relational crisis state.

Monday night at Rev. class, I saw something that helped me to connect the dots. You know how when you're in love, the things you see in that person that appear to be odd, you see as adorable and cute? He has some odd mannerisms and facial expressions, and they did appear childish when I was in love with him, yet I classified them as part of his peculiar sense of humor. He would always try to get a laugh, and he'd succeed. But this past Monday, I looked at his behaviors for what they were... peculiar! And further classifying them, they were outright childlike! He just seemed like a big kid, and it looked so out of place. Boy... love really does put blinders on you! For two years, I would not call it what it was, because I loved him so. But Dick is very childlike in his ways and in his mannerisms. He is not a masculine man. For a while, before I fell in love with him, I wondered if what I was seeing was effeminate behavior. But once he started pursing a relationship with me, he put on more manly behavior.

So I'm thinking that perhaps those peculiar and un-masculine ways stem more from his being childlike more so than effeminate. He is really just a real tall boy! His mannerisms all betray that. And his behaviors really betray that... even to others. Three friends who met him before we married held their tongues, but after we split they shared that he was "questionable" to them. [That's why it's important to solicit friends' honest opinions before even getting engaged! Unfortunately, I didn't.] And other friends I've confided in lately have used the words, "...peculiar," "not manly," and "not a real man," when giving their honest opinion of him. Yet another friend pointed out that he has irresponsible behavior, such as when he blew off our friends' wedding RSVP without letting them (or me) know ahead of time. Or when he was scheduled to teach kids' Sunday school, but just didn't show up, since he was avoiding repaying me. We're all assessing the same thing. Dick is irresponsible and refuses to take on adult responsibility.

So, when an adult refuses to take seriously his adult responsibilities, and when his behavior is more childlike than adult, and when he avoids accountability, this can only lead to demise at some point. And when you throw a marriage into the mix, there is no way it (or they – three marriages for Dick) is going to last. No woman is going to put up with that. Marriage is difficult enough, but when you realize you're married to a child, the prospect is either to wait for him to grow into a man, or to get out. Three have opted out!

Now, I must give him credit for taking his parental responsibilities seriously. That's good. But perhaps because he's still a boy, being a husband is just too tall an order for him. Boys shouldn't get married. His mom even told him that he should not remarry. He claimed she didn't share why, but I suspect that this is the reason.

His spiritual crisis is self-inflicted. All the scriptures that I referenced state that there are spiritual repercussions to our decisions to disobey God's word and way. So, the result is a spiritual crisis. He may not see the beginnings of it yet, but he has opened up the floodgates to God's promises. Unfortunately, these are promises of loss, not gain. His spiritual crisis means that he will suffer loss in his future. Just the loss of God not answering his prayers is loss enough! And his tithes and gift-giving will be for naught – just as if he weren't giving at all.

Then add to his spiritual crisis some faulty theology. He takes the "name-it-claim-it" teaching to a whole new level! He believes Christians don't get sick: "Don't admit you have the illness. Don't call it by its name, because that's a confession that you have it!" Never mind that God says in His word that He heals us; that must mean that Christians do get sick! Well, because of this faulty theology he embraces, he keeps canceling his doctors' appointments. He went from April through July canceling and rescheduling his endocrine specialist's appointments. He finally went in July (I went with him, even though we had separated), but then he canceled his follow-up appointment, since he didn't like the doctor's diagnosis. So his behavior has landed him in a health crisis too! I had actually emailed his mom after our separation to inform her of his health crisis and to see if she could urge him to stop postponing and canceling his doctor appointments. I never got a response from her.

Dick is a runner; he runs from responsibility. He lacks the "ability" to "respond" correctly; hence, the lack of "response-ability". He doesn't want to be held accountable. It is his M.O.; Dick has a habit of running from accountability, whether it is counseling sessions where he'd have to account for his actions, or doctors' appointments where he'd have to account for a disease that he will not acknowledge. He refuses to claim responsibility, even for his own health. This is the ultimate sacrifice. Wow! This is bordering on mental illness. Now that's a thought!

### Chapter 20: NO JUDGMENT!

*Thursday, December 18th, 2014*

*I've been thinking about how Christians spend more time judging other Christians than being a witness to unbelievers. There's this one-size-fits-all notion of Christian life – that if* we're faithful and obedient, things will go well. Thus, if things aren't going well, then we must not be faithful and obedient. This thinking is especially true of those who have had great long-termed marriages. But just because God brought them their mates and things worked great, doesn't mean it will happen that way for everyone. There is no heavenly "cookie-cutter" to meeting and marrying a great guy and having a great marriage! Not to say that great marriages are great due to lack of marital problems. No; all marriages will have problems. It's just that if both parties are willing, marital problems can be overcome. But some marriages never had that potential because they were never great matches from the start, or because one party isn't really willing to put in the work to make it work.

In those cases, the other party is trapped. Others counseling them to "stay and pray" don't realize that this person is in a relationship with a party who doesn't want the marriage. And yes, we should pray for softened hearts and changed behavior. Yet we know that some will, and some won't. And for those who won't, God didn't fail to answer prayer; that party just failed to answer to God! So, just let the one in that situation use their own wisdom to move on if they find themselves married to someone who won't participate in the marriage!

I'm reminded of a friend's counsel to me when I informed her that Dick and I are going through a divorce. She immediately went into that "stay and pray" mode! She knew nothing at the time, so I decided to clue her in to just the financial fraud. She still wouldn't get off that mode. I finally told her about the sexual fraud, and she said, "Well, there are women whose husbands run into ED issues after years of marriage, and they shouldn't just leave." Wow, she just doesn't get it! And she wouldn't. This woman has been married to a great guy for over 30 years. Over the years, she has attested to how wonderful a husband he is. And she has had the fortune of being able to roll over on any and every night of her life for the past 30 plus years and make love to her husband. She has never known a drought! Yet she's telling me that I should endure a lifelong drought.

But she's missing the main points. First, my husband committed fraud; he deceived me from before we were married. He knew he had ED issues, but failed to disclose them. Secondly, and therfore, we were not able to consummate the marriage; so there is no marriage. Thirdly, he refused to try to solve his issues with medical intervention. So, waiting more years for things to improve would have been for naught. What I had suspected to be diabetes and the resultant ED would only get worse untreated; not better. So she's trying to confine me to a celibate marriage. Fourthly, due to his impotence, he practiced avoidance behavior with me with regards to any intimacy or affection. "Don't start nothing, won't be nothing," was his approach. So he had cut off our affection connection, which had been the entire lifeline of our relationship.

But let me add a fifth, not so obvious point. Let me flip the script on her. I wish that I could ask her for her response to this scenario. No, let me ask any woman what she thinks any husband's response to this would be. So, ladies, let's say that a man had fallen in love with and married a lady with whom he'd been abstinent. On their wedding night, he finds out that her vagina had been sewn up! She is confused as to why he's startled, perturbed, upset, hurt, angry, etc. She replies, "We're still in love; we can still hug and kiss; we can even spoon naked now that we're married!" Hubby's still dumbfounded, so he doesn't reply! She goes on to say that it was a medical necessity when she was younger, but the doctor assured her that she can be artificially inseminated, and that she can deliver by cesarean. "So no worries, we can still have babies!" He's still dumbfounded! Then she says, "I don't see what the fuss is about; we still have a marriage!" He finally replies that he was hoping for sexual intimacy with her, the rest of his life. She responds, "We can do everything except for having intercourse; and we can spoon the rest of our lives!"

What do you think his response would be? He's getting out of there! No heterosexual man is going to stay in a marriage where he can't have intercourse with his wife — from the beginning and forever! But here's the double standard: women are expected to if their husbands can't perform. Yes, I agree; if this happens later, stay and work with him through whatever treatments are necessary. But not if he defrauded you and then refuses help!

Okay, last scenario. This one is for a woman. Let's say that you marry this great guy. The love of your life! You've been looking forward to marrying him and finally loving him in an intimate manner. You get married, and on your wedding night, you discover that he is a "she"! Yes! This is a transgender person who had undergone hormonal treatment and surgical alterations rendering an underperforming penis. Let me just use the same adverbs I used above. You are startled, perturbed, upset, hurt, angry, etc. He replies, "We're still in love; we can still hug and kiss; we can even spoon naked, now that we're married!" You're still dumbfounded! He goes on to say, "I thought it didn't matter because we love each other!" You're still dumbfounded, so you don't reply. Then he says, "I don't see what the fuss is about; we still have a marriage!" You finally reply that you were hoping for sexual intimacy with him, the rest of your life. He responds, "We can do everything except for having intercourse; and we can spoon the rest of our lives!"

So, ladies, would you buy that? Would you "stay and pray"? I don't think so; you'd be "so out of there"! But for some reason, some think that I should endure the rest of my life with someone who defrauded me and can't and won't make love to me! Some would say it's different. Well, no - fraud is fraud, and the result is still the same. The result is like being in bed with a woman or a transgender woman/man!

Christian people! We must stop persecuting other Christians! Christians who have to make really tough life-choices don't need you to make it worse by making them feel guilty! It is not your business. You are not saving a soul here! They are already saved. You're just meddling! You are advising them on life-long painful decisions, and then you go home and enjoy the very thing you've advised them to go without! Don't be a hypocrite like the Pharisees! Yes, they too thought they were giving sound, spiritual advice. But Jesus called them out on it and revealed their legalism. They were adhering to the letter of the law, not the spirit of the law. Jesus came with grace and mercy, whereas, the law was created to point us to a need for grace and mercy, because the law cannot be obeyed by every human at every moment. So, Jesus brings with Him not only salvation, but a new covenant, based on His blood and grace and mercy. So if Jesus Christ can have mercy, then those who are called by His name – Christians – should have mercy!

Jesus also said in Romans 8 that there is no condemnation in Jesus: "There is therefore now no condemnation to them which are in Christ Jesus, who walk not after the flesh, but after the Spirit. For the law of the Spirit of life in Christ Jesus hath made me free from the law of sin and death." Jesus Christ doesn't condemn me, and I shouldn't let Christians condemn me either.

Choosing not to stay married under those or other conditions is between the person and the Lord. Even choosing to have a sexual relationship with one's partner outside of marriage is also between that person and the Lord. As it goes with judgmental Christians: damned if you do, damned if you don't and end up divorcing! They either judge you on the front end for pre-marital sex, or on the back end for divorcing! So each person should live out their Christian walk and not judge others'. Our commission is to go out and make disciples of the nations, not to go condemning other Christians!

*As I was sharing my change of marital status with a particular single friend, I didn't get a judgmental response. She just wanted to know more, so I shared the 411. Her eyes opened real wide, and she shared that the man she is dating wants to get married, and he has diabetes. She too, practices abstinence, and so of course she was very alarmed at the possibility... She said that she is going to ask him if he is able to achieve erections. I told her that he could just lie. In fact, he could be in denial, as Dick was. I mean, we would be lying there naked and engaged in foreplay with no erection (or shall I call it "instead-of -play"), and Dick would still say he wasn't impotent! He'd say that I just hadn't stimulated him enough! He denied his ED to his wife, so of course this* gentleman could deny it to his girlfriend! She retorted then that she'd just ask him to show it to her! More power to you girl! And I wouldn't be one of those Christians who'd say not to have sex with him either. It is not my business!

Until yesterday, I was the only person I knew of who unknowingly married an impotent man. But as I was praying with another Christian friend of mine, she intimated to me that her last two divorces were over this same issue! She married two men, back to back, who failed to disclose that they were impotent! It's amazing! That is one of the most self-centered things a man can do! Have a Christian woman who loves you to bind herself to you for life, though you have no intention or ability of ever having a sex-life with her! She is just tough-out-of-luck! And he claims he loves her? This is not love! This is finding someone who didn't expect sex from you prior to marriage and who you think won't divorce you after the secret is out! That is one of the most un-loving and selfish things a person can do! It is utterly appalling! I guess there is a sub-culture of impotent men who are going around doing this. I wish they'd just find in-the-closet lesbians to hook up with!

Speaking of which, there is also a sub-culture of in-the-closet homosexual men who marry unsuspecting Christian women who had been abstinent. Over my lifetime, I have known of many faithful Christian women who inadvertently married gay men, and then divorced them; enough to count on two hands! This is unspeakable! We can't put ourselves in this position!

Well, back to my point: this dear friend of mine had the misfortune to have this happen once, but then she made choices that opened the door to a repeat occurrence. Now, I have to admit that I actually didn't learn from my first marriage either; which, for the record, wasn't a case of ED. No, the problem with the first marriage was that, since we had not had any physical connection prior to marriage, I did not know that he was not affectionate. He was a strong believer who practiced abstinence, so he told me that he was just withholding affection to keep from getting aroused. In fact, we didn't kiss until in front of the altar for this very reason! But once we got home, I remember putting my arms around him and trying to kiss him, and he wouldn't! I said, "It's all right now; we're married now, you can kiss me." He said he is just not affectionate! I was dumbfounded! I replied that he can get used to getting and giving affection. He replied, "Well, I'd just be doing that because you want it, not because I want to give it!" Dumbfounded again, I said, "What's wrong with doing something for your wife just because she wants it?" Yes, within week one of our wedding, he retorted, "I'm not going to do something for you because you want it. If I do something for you, it will be because I want to do it!" Yes, from week one, our marriage was doomed! Though we did have intercourse, we never made love a single time in ten years of marriage! Two beautiful children came out of that union though.

But I didn't learn enough from that situation. I thought that as long as my next fiancé and I were affectionate without pre-marital sex, this would avert any affection and *sexual problems when married. I also thought that since God knew that though I was celibate, I wanted a good sex life in my marriage, He'd handle that part (that "God Dust" theory!). Well apparently this isn't true. I'm not blaming God; I'm actually blaming myself for not using the head that He gave me. And I blame myself for listening to all the condemners who act like pre-marital sex is the unforgivable sin!*

I should have used more discretion in making such a life-long decision. I frankly feel that I have done more harm by discrediting marriage with such a short-term marriage and divorce, than had I indulged in pre-marital sex (or tried to), and then determined not to marry him based on what I found. If marriage is so sacred and it's supposed to last forever, I should have been more diligent in making sure that I had crossed all my "t's" and dotted my "i's". I should have covered all my bases. We all know that the two leading causes of divorce are sex issues and finances. And these are exactly the two areas that ruined us! I did nothing to examine these two areas to make sure that we were sound. We didn't have sex before we married, and we didn't go through extensive counseling that would have covered finances and other topics.

One would think that God would honor the "good sex" part, since we were "good" and didn't have sex prior to marriage. But it is apparent that this isn't true. My friend and I both had two marriages, each with no love making! In three of these cases, there was no physical ability to make love, and in one, there was physical ability, but no emotional ability.

I have really come to the conclusion that if God doesn't take care of that component, then he really does expect us to. This flies in the face of everything we've been taught, but I have two real experiences that tell me that God doesn't just sprinkle "God Dust" on your marriage to make the sex component good. You have to have determined that for yourself. And if He "hates divorce" so much and He knows that sex issues are the leading cause of divorce, then He must want us to get that component right.

Christians talk like divorce is the second worst sin (with fornication being the first). Many are so quick to quote, "God hates divorce!" But God hates bad marriages too! So again, since bad sex makes for bad marriages, He must want us to have explored that area to make sure that we get it right in the first place. That's my opinion, not my advocacy. That's my understanding that I took out of this marriage – No Judgment!

Well, if that's the case, then could God really mean what we've been taught that He means about premarital-sex? This question drove me to research the topic. In doing so, I did discover that the original Greek scriptures that dealt with prohibited sex used a word that had several meanings, including harlotry and idolatry. But when these particular scriptures were translated centuries ago, one term was used to cover all sex outside of marriage – instead of using terms identifying just the disdainful sexual behaviors – and that term was "fornication".

If you look up the word "fornication" in the dictionary, it does state our generally accepted meaning of "pre-marital sex". But I'd rather go with what God means than what Mr. Webster says. I'll go with the generally accepted Bible-study convention of using the original Greek meaning as the truth. And using His original terminology, God prohibited a particular set of sexual practices, and we'd have to do further study to learn what lies within this set.

[So why didn't the translators seek to maintain the original meaning and use the appropriate wording in context? Perhaps the intended meaning was widened to the all-encompassing term, "fornication", to control the sexual behavior of the masses over the centuries. I was recently speaking with my friend, Teresa, who had done extensive research on the topic and found that St. Jerome was responsible for this loose translation centuries ago. In speculating about why, I threw this out there: there could have been a venereal disease outbreak at the time (and no cure), and he wanted to end all sex outside of marriage to limit the spread! Or, what if the term "lasciviousness", which is used in some verses (defined as lewd sexual acts and thoughts), were the more appropriate translation in most verses where we find the translation, "fornication". And since some may not have deemed their sexual activities as lewd, then St. Jerome might have found it expedient to just ban all pre-marital relations with the translation, "fornication".

This is kind of like when you hear preachers preach against going to parties. In their own past "sin-lives", partying might have included drugs and promiscuity. They probably don't realize that there are many who don't associate dancing at a party with any of these activities; therefore, going to a club to enjoy some dancing is not a sin for them. But for those for whom partying meant drugs and promiscuity, going to the club is a huge temptation; and thus for them it may be a sin. But for Christians and pastors to give everyone the same restriction of never stepping into a club or party due to their own past struggles is unfair and unnecessary, and frankly, unbiblical. To give a blanket condemnation of clubs, parties and dancing so as to minimize the likelihood of running into drugs and sex is overkill; but it is exactly what some churches preach. BTW, I don't go to clubs or parties where drug use and sex are taking place; I just go to legit places. And yes, alcohol is being served there; but again, many believers have used the overkill approach to alcohol. The Bible says not to be drunk with wine. There was no admonishment never to drink it; we all know that Jesus turned water into wine... so some consumption is fine. The sin is in getting drunk or high, rendering your control to the prince of this earth... the enemy.

Well perhaps in the same way, St. Jerome used the overkill approach to pre-marital sex, via his chosen translation. Maybe he just chose to kill all pre-marital sex rather than specifying all the perversions that God hates. Just like many preachers do today by preaching that drinking is a sin, even though it is clear in the Bible that it isn't, perhaps St. Jerome decided to choose a more absolute term, "fornication", than a relative term, "lasciviousness". Maybe, for ease of translation, he just used the broadest most prohibitive term, which means total abstinence, except for those married!

Of course we don't know for sure! This is just my quandary and resultant questions; I'm not saying that this is spirit led inspiration and revelation. But Teresa and I have talked about writing a follow-up book after we've done much more research on the topic (years from now). But let me make it clear that I am not stating that Christians should change their abstinence conviction (especially for teens and young adults); and I am certainly not advocating promiscuity at all! Abstinence is better than promiscuity, which is probably what St. Jerome was thinking...]

*Well my friend who is dating the diabetic who wants to marry her is in her 50's and has never been married. It would make no sense for her to have been single and celibate for many years, waiting on the right man, and end up married to someone with whom she'll have to spend the rest of her life celibate, or end up in a quick divorce! Let's use our heads people! There should be no condemnation from Christians for women experiencing this aspect of their relationships ahead of time, especially as we age and our partners age. ED issues are more prominent in older men, especially those who are diabetic. So, middle-aged buyers beware! Buyers, be smart! You might want to at least squeeze the fruit, because once you take him home, he's yours!*

## Chapter 21: IT'S NOT OVER YET!

*Friday, December 26th, 2014*

*Well, Dick never called to reschedule the mediation; surprise! But this reinforced what I learned about prayer. We can pray that God moves on someone's heart and soften it, but we can't expect a certain action to definitely take place, because God gave man a volitional mind. Man can change it at the last minute, even if God has moved on their heart to do something. So it isn't a matter of God failing; it is a matter of man failing to do God's will. It is like the Genie telling a person that they can ask for anything, except making a person fall in love. God is able, but not willing to override man's will. God is able, but man is not always willing!*

Dick never did plan to meet with Jheri and me. In fact, I received a text from Dr. Z. that Dick wanted to meet with him (not with Jheri). Dr. Z. said that if Dick wants to include me in a meeting, then it's at Dick's discretion; he will let us know. This actually infuriated me, because I don't understand why there is so much tolerance for a man who betrayed me and has taken six months already, four of which were since Dr. Z. first texted him to offer counsel. Over this period, Dr. Z. would always tell me that Dick just needs more time, or that he's just hurting. Why does he get such a long rope? And meanwhile, Dr. Z. knows that Dick has left me with a financial burden. No, I don't expect Dr. Z. to make Dick talk to him; but why excuse his behavior? This is enabling behavior, which I wouldn't expect from a counselor.

This happened a couple of days after I last saw them at a semi-formal Christmas party where Dr. Z. was being honored. I had been asked to give the welcome, but unbeknownst to me, they had asked Dick to do the scripture reading. When he entered, although I was already seated, he chose to sit at another table. When he was to read the scripture, he talked extensively and emotionally about the scripture first. He was really into it, and it made me think about how hypocritical he truly is. No one there would know that this man who was sounding like a preacher had stiffed someone in that audience, his wife, for $11k! [It's ironic that the exact same amount that he owes me, between pre-marital financial obligations ($6k) and marital debt ($5k), is what he was so willing to pay his ex in arrears that technically should have been reduced during his unemployed years!]

## NARRATIVE

[I thought that this would be the end of my journal... again! But there were more chapters in my journey. 2014 was just about through, and I was completely through with Dick and the possibility of being on any friendly terms. Dick had passed up the chances he had been given to make things right, and it would be just a matter of time before the court system was to make a judgment on the debt he is to repay. I thought that whenever the judgment and divorce decree came, I'd just jot it down in my journal and journal no more! Boy was I wrong! The last few weeks of the year, I had let the hurt and pain of betrayal get to me at my soul, where my body recognizes it! It ain't over!!!!!!]

# PHASE 5 – "IT'S ALL GOOD!"

## Chapter 22: "A WAKE-UP CALL!"

**Sunday, January 11th, 2015**

Wow! I would never have guessed how I'd spend New Year's Eve! In the hospital! Yes... ER! I had a mild stroke! I can't believe the words when I hear myself speak them, or see it in print! I literally brought in my new year with three mini-strokes. On the 31st, I had a TIA, and on January 2nd I had a stroke, followed by another TIA the next day!

But I refuse to look at it as a negative. I see it as my wake-up call. I see it as my life-line; a life-preserver thrown out to me as I was being swept down the stream of destruction of life... or quality of life. I was dancing with the "Silent-Killer" – hypertension. I had allowed myself to live with unmanaged stage 1 hypertension for many years. Doctors had not challenged it with different prescriptions; they just kept increasing my dosage. They said things like, "Well maybe this is your norm," or, "Since you are hypertensive, these higher numbers are fine." This is utterly ridiculous! High numbers are never fine, and as I now know, they can lead to stroke in a person who, "takes care of herself"! A skinny person with hypertension is more at stroke risk than an overweight person without it! End of story! Don't get it twisted! Obesity is just a risk factor predisposing a person to hypertension, which itself, is the culprit. If, although predisposed, the obese person doesn't have hypertension, then he or she is not at as much stroke risk as the skinny person with hypertension!

I thought that I had taken really good care of myself with my good eating habits and regular workouts. But in fact, since good lifestyle wasn't enough for me, then taking care of myself should have included making the doctors give me meds that work for me! Five hours of cardio weekly, three weekly yoga classes, weight machines and right eating could not replace the lowering effect of the three meds that I am now on to manage my blood pressure. So, the way to take care of one's self is to reduce the numbers. If exercise and right eating don't do it, then meds should!

[I want to emphasize what I wrote at that point. You must be an advocate for your own health. The doctors had not switched up my meds to see what worked better... they just kept increasing the dosage of one that didn't work. This is crazy! Even after the stroke, the three meds they prescribed weren't consistently lowering my blood pressure, so months later I insisted that they try two completely different classes of meds. They work!]

But the final straw was stress and anxiety. They say that stress kills, but I hadn't realized how stressed out that farce of a marriage had really made me. The fraud and his treatment of me were bad enough, but then the betrayal after we separated was the final dagger! But I thought that I was coping with it. Maybe emotionally and spiritually I was, but already being stage 1 hypertensive, physically, my body was not able to handle the additional stress and anxiety. I didn't know!

[I want to add something very important here. Heart disease is the number one killer of women. I've known of women younger than I, dying of strokes and heart attacks, and you probably know some as well. And in a lot of these cases, these women appeared to be in good health. But stress kills even the healthy! That's what women need to realize! Unhealthy relationships (whether with men or your job) produce unhealthy bodies, via stress! We cannot continue in unhealthy relationships, because the body recognizes the stress even when the mind hasn't quite identified it! And even if you do recognize it and deal with it, by then, it may be too late! Ladies, qualify your partner before you make him your partner for life! Don't take on anyone who doesn't have your best interest at heart, because eventually, his insincere actions will affect your heart... emotionally, physically or both!]

I've been doing more reflecting, but I am just not feeling up to journaling about it; but I thank God that I am able to enter this! I'm still somewhat weak, but thank God that there are no residuals... no short or long-term damage to any functions! I thank God!

Sunday, March 1st, 2015

Here I am, two months post-TIAs and stroke! Hallelujah! I have full use of my hands and fingers to key my journal entries! I have full use of my legs and other body functions and I'm stronger! Hallelujah! Thank you, Father! And I have to give much appreciation to Jeanine, who stepped up and took real good care of her mom – buying groceries and cooking three meals a day for me for a month! Thanks also to Jeremy and Jeanine for the trips to the doctor. And I would be remiss if I didn't thank my friends and my POG family for the hospital visits and the meals that you brought me at home while I was recovering. And to my cousin, Ethel, and friend, Sharon, who still check up on me with their regular calls; and to my friend, Regena, who continues to bring me food, even until now... thanks a million!

I give God the glory for His marvelous intervention in my life with an eye-opener; a wakeup call... a life-saver! Yes, He threw out the life-line when I was floating down the rapids of unmanaged hypertension, headed towards the waterfall of stroke or heart disease. I never thought I'd be talking about a stroke that I had, but thank God for it, because it was mild enough to cause no impairments and leave no residuals! It was a wakeup call about my hypertension! It closed the door to my ignorance about my hypertension and opened the door, yes, via a stroke, to better management of my health – better healthcare and better stress management!

I'm back to myself... actually, I was back five weeks ago, but my stamina was very low. It built up over the last three or so weeks, but then it started waning again and my blood pressure started fluctuating again. It has gone up to 150/110 and as low as 110/66, awake and walking! I do pray that it normalizes to the one-teens over mid-70's. Tonight I go to our healing service, and I pray dear Lord, that you send a complete healing. In Jesus' name, Amen!

## IT'S IN HIS HANDS!

So, I was kinda out of touch with my regular journaling for that period, but... I'm back! There has been no movement on the divorce. I gave it to God to fight the battle. It was the stress of my heaviness of heart over my husband's betrayal that tipped the scale, making my blood pressure sky-rocket. So I can't afford to make the mistake of thinking about it anymore. I won't even spend any more time praying on it, because that would mean that I'm thinking about it. I have already prayed. God knows, and God has my best interest in His plans. He does have a plan! So Lord, I surrender my plan, and I look expectantly to You to bring this mess to a close; I pray that You'd restore me... my heart, my soul, my spirit, my trust, my finances, my time, and my health! In Jesus' name, Amen!

So, since my book is a compilation of my journal reflections about the failed marriage and my revelations and resolutions, and since those are complete, then it is time to construct my book. I am going to finish this book this month! [So, I thought!] However, there are still revelations that come to me through things I hear, see and mostly the Holy Spirit revealing to me. So I will continue to do entries, such as:

## DISFUNCTIONAL JUSTIFICATION!

Jheri called me on Wednesday, 2/25, and I believe the Holy Spirit led her to call. After asking how I was doing, she said she was watching "Iyanla: Fix My Life", and there was a pastor on who had been married for 20 years and is now telling his wife that he really never wanted to be married to her! He wouldn't tell his real secret, besides addiction to porn, but he has one. She spoke of how some men marry as a cover, and I shared that I believe this was the case with Dick! She also talked about how some men marry a woman to get back at their ex. I believe this too applies. I recalled the time we were exiting the gym where his son had finished a basketball game, and we happened to be in front of his ex. He grabbed my hand, and I felt it was odd, since he doesn't display affection. It occurred to me that it was for her "benefit". I think of the fact that since he had such a public break-up with his ex, and that his mom even said that he shouldn't remarry, that he is still not healed from that marriage and was nowhere near ready to take on another marriage. So I was just there to get back at her. He never intended to love me or stay with me. And he certainly never intended on making love to me!

Jheri talked about how in her practice she sees it... a man messing over the life of a beautiful, educated wife, just for his dysfunctional justification... leaving her totally devastated! Well, he almost left me in that state, but I won't let him exile me to another state... of ill health! I'm staying here, and he's exiled! Out of my life, out of my house, out of my mind! And Lord, I need him out of my dreams too! Last month, I woke up one morning and realized that he had been in my dream. I was appalled, and then finally, Stan was in my dreams, so I felt that marked the end of my ex being in my subconscious.

## MARCH FORTH!

*Wednesday, March 4th, 2015*

On this day, I MARCH FORTH INTO VICTORY! I started my victory march by initiating the actual compilation of my book!

*Friday, May 1st, 2015*

Wow! It's exactly one year ago that I started journaling! A lot has changed! But emotionally, a lot has stayed the same. How I let it get to May 1st before I picked up my laptop to journal again since March, I don't know – but I'm back! I know that part of the delay was returning to the topic... the "mess". But I am a positive person, so I will let the "message" be what draws me back and keeps me back until this message is finished. Also, I've been enjoying my new found increased energy as of late and I'm trying to be productive in other areas.

### "YOUTUBE UNIVERSITY"

Predominantly, that area has been health research. I've been a student of "YouTube University"! My search for "natural" solutions to hypertension just led me to more and more YouTube videos and Google searches. So I've been at it for about eight weeks straight! It has been so productive; I've actually learned a great deal. At first I found nothing on the causes of hypertension. All the searches led to the same thing. Doctors claim to not know what causes it; they only state that diet and exercise can help. Well I'm already on top of that. But the moment I used search phrases such as "natural alternatives" or "holistic approach", the flood-gates opened up. I not only learned the various root causes of hypertension, but the remedies.

[I would be remiss if I didn't share some of my findings with you. Increased blood pressure results from vascular constriction, which can result from decreasing amounts of nitric oxide in our arteries either as we age or for other reasons. The supplements, L-Arginine and L-Citrulline boost nitric oxide levels, resulting in vasodilation, thus decreasing blood pressure. There are so many brands of L-Arginine on the market sold as a work-out enhancement. I avoided those and purchased from Arginine Essentials. Their web site showed that much research was put into their formulation, and its intended use is optimized cardio-vascular health, not better work-outs. I, however, felt that my hypertension was more menopause related, not nitric oxide related, so I continued my quest for natural remedies that directly addressed the root issue.]

I also did a lot of reading. In mid-March, my boyfriend sent me a book called "Why Is Mid-life Mooching Your Mojo?" by Dr. Joni Labbe who is a functional doctor. This book surprisingly seemed to have all the answers, because it seemed to target a lot of potential problems of menopausal women. A lot of mid-life health issues are interrelated, which can be good, because the same solutions seem to address and fix many issues!

[For years, I had thought that my hypertension was linked to menopause. In fact, I'm reminded of a statement I heard at the wellness study group that I joined this year at the African America Museum of Beginnings in Pomona. Health educator, Cheyenne English told us that she had challenged her doctor saying, "My body's on fire from menopause, and you mean to tell me that it isn't the reason for my hypertension?" We know our own bodies, and we have to seek our own answers! I knew that my constant severe hot flashes sent my adrenals into overdrive over the years, affecting my blood pressure; but medical doctors weren't buying that!]

*Dr. Labbe talked about less conventional testing protocols that medical doctors don't even know exist. Of course such tests; alternative or functional doctor visits; and prescribed supplementation or treatment are not covered by health insurance. This is so ironic, because I truly do believe that health problems are caused by a nutritional deficiency, not a medication deficiency! Yet "health" insurance doesn't cover natural solutions! So basically, they're insuring the "health" of "Big-Pharma's" profit margin! The "health care" industry should call itself the "symptom management" industry instead!*

[This book led me to take a saliva test which proved my suspicions that my constant, intense hot-flashes overworked my adrenals, flooding my system with excess cortisol which kept me in the fight-or-flight mode, resulting in vasoconstriction, hence hypertension. The adaptogenic herb, Ashwaganda was recommended by Dr. Labbe for balancing the adrenal glands. I take a product by Himalaya called Stress Care that contains Ashwaganda and other herbs designed to normalize cortisol levels. It makes a tremendous difference in my state of calm, hence it keeps my blood pressure from rising. Nature's Way, Calm Aid also seems to work on my sympathetic nervous system, resulting in vasodilation. I also read that one of my meds depletes melatonin levels in the body, so I replenish it with melatonin supplements that also aid in sleep.

Another thing to keep an eye on is the big downward spiraling effect of mid-life symptoms and the resultant prescribed medications. Menopause or mid-life may lead to high blood pressure, then blood pressure meds may deplete your melatonin levels, making your hot-flash induced insomnia even worse; then the doctor prescribes hormone replacement therapy (HRT) for the hot-flashes, but HRT should never be taken by a woman with high blood pressure! There are many other herbal recommendations in Dr. Labbe's book that address mid-life health issues at the root – upstream, where the problem starts, not downstream, where medical doctors treat the symptoms with medications that can spiral you downward. However, it is advisable to continue blood pressure meds unless your medical doctor weans you off, even if your alternative protocol is sustaining a healthy blood pressure.]

## Chapter 23: PEELING THAT STINKY ONION!

*May 4th, 2015*

On Sunday, April 26th, I woke up early with a lot on my mind. It was that subject again... how I got with such a looser who turned my world upside-down in such a short period of time! Even just writing this brought down my spirit, which is why I didn't journal this until now, May 4th. But I must journal it, because my introspection that day led me to some productive conclusions.

As I lay there, I became aware of a sense of mourning, and tears were coming down. So then I tuned into what my thoughts were, and there they were again — those thoughts of how wrong Dick had done me. How he just walked into my life and flipped it upside down and walked right out, leaving emotional, financial and health repercussions. The man did nothing to improve my life. He added no iota of betterment, enjoyment, fulfillment, etc. He only took from me. He took a lot, and I am still in mourning. Not over losing him, but over my collateral damage! It is amazing to think that my life was going along sooooo well, and yet I allowed a person to walk in, align himself to me, then devastate me and come out the better! He used me as his financial "cover", hence, he saved a lot of money while with me; got a "cover" for whatever he was covering up; got hooked up with two wonderful local ministries and steppin' lessons; lived in a nice place; got a free vacation, free tires, all his meals cooked for him and brought to him; got his clothes and home cleaned; and didn't even have to buy the wedding ring!

Me, I got smacked upside the head with the biggest surprise a new wife could find – her husband is impotent! Then I learned that he didn't plan on contributing to half of the household expenses. Add to that – he couldn't be "husband" on weekends he was "father"; most of the time he wouldn't even attempt to have sex; wouldn't try to get medical intervention; was cheap – he never, ever bought me a gift when married; he wouldn't do the work he used to do when we were dating; he snored, keeping me awake; he wouldn't repay me for my financial losses that he caused; he wouldn't continue in counseling, etc. But what followed our separation was worse. He betrayed me! He left all that unpaid debt on me and never repaid a dime! And the financial strain and emotional drain resulted in a stroke!

I can now see that I am still carrying around the emotional burden of the devastation Dick left in his wake, because I woke up with it on my mind, crying. This made me realize that the wound is far deeper than I had thought, and that Dick had hurt me down to my soul! Although I wasn't pining away for him and had realized what a snake he was, this didn't mean that I could just swiftly sweep it under the rug. I said "good riddance", but I'm only rid of "him", not the devastation! It obviously is taking many months to heal.

We've now been separated more months than we'd been married, and I'm not even close to being healed! This is because it is not just a head wound, or a heart wound. This man hurt me down to my SOUL! He devastated me! He tore up my sense of hope in a future marriage, trust in men, and trust in Christians to do the right thing; not to mention leaving me a tremendous amount of debt to deal with on a retirement income. In fact, my friend, Marthenia, used this term "soul wound" earlier this year when I called her to tell her about the stroke. She sensed that I had been hurt down to the soul and ministered to me. [Minister Marthenia Satterfield of Purpose Path Network, Int.]

So, with all these emotions of devastation swimming around in my heart, mind and soul, it is no wonder that I woke up tearing and feeling blue. These feelings are deeply rooted down in my soul. I didn't just get blindsided by this man in my past, but he has colored the way I see relationships in my future. This is because he fooled me soooooo well! Anyone who meets this man thinks that he is Jesus Jr.! He portrays himself to be so meek and kind and Christlike and wonderful! I soooo fell for this – and married this – and was the biggest fool ever! So how can I trust my judgment going forward? Never mind looking back at the pain and devastation; what about my future? What he did to me has ramifications on my expectations for my future. How can I ever let a man come into my life again, since I obviously don't know the difference between rotten fruit and good fruit? The theme of my life is now – "I was fooled, and so now I'm a fool!"

*He played the biggest, meanest game on me, and so now I'm a fool and can't trust my judgment anymore.*

*Well thank God that I don't have to trust my judgment. He had a plan with a man named Stan, who was already in my life! He's a man I've been trusting for ages as a friend. [I just thought of this, but I've known Marthenia and Stan for about the same amount of time; I met them both in high school!] Thank God! But I don't know how I missed the mark with not hearing from God to choose Stan over Dick. I had so many people, both strangers and those in my life, give me "Word of Knowledge" about Dick being the right one, but boy were they wrong! And it isn't just a matter of a relationship going sour! It was bad from the start, from before we wed. He conned me from the time he got me to purchase my own wedding ring with no intentions of paying me back, and from the moment he proposed, knowing that he was impotent! This marriage never should have taken place!*

So, I'm feeling wounded and like a fool! Compounded emotions with big ramifications! I realized I still had some emotions to sort through and give up to God. So I lay there before church, just letting the sad thoughts and tears flow. I peeled another layer off that stinky onion. My next realization that Sunday morning was that I still hadn't let go of the deeply rooted wish that Dick would straighten up and do right by me. Though he hadn't in ten months, I still held out hope, because after all... this is God's wish for all mankind... to do right by others. So for Dick to repent and repay would not only mean that I get repaid, but it would complete a much bigger picture. I needed to see him do right – period – to redeem my hope in man! It was too painful for me all at once to lose my marriage, lose the hope of restoration of my brother, the hope of restoration of funds, and the hope of being able to trust in a man! So as a defense mechanism unbeknownst to me, I had only let go of one of these at a time.

I let go of him as my husband in June and July 2014, but I truly had hoped that we could be amicable. But in September I finally acknowledged that he was definitely the swindler that I suspected he was, and so I filed for divorce. I went through October thinking that I was fine and that it was all behind me, but in November, reality set in that I wasn't over it. The large debt he stuck me with was a constant reminder, and his prevailing at our court hearing let me know a fight was ahead. But mostly, it was the gnawing thought that this man really intended me harm and never meant any good in my life! I had been giving him the benefit of the doubt all these months, but deep inside, I knew that he was never innocent... as he tries to appear. He was guilty from the beginning of never intending to carry even half the financial weight, and for him to stop the repayment the moment he left meant he had only been slowly repaying me when we were married because he needed to keep a roof over his head! The moment that was not an issue, he stopped the repayment!

But back to my timeline of peeling that stinky onion, in December, Jheri put it on my heart to fully forgive him by praying that he comes into repentance. She offered to meet with us as a mediator, we prayed about it, and he agreed to a meeting. But he canceled it the day of and would not reschedule it. I, on the other hand, had taken this too much to heart, literally. I took this seriously, because it meant his reparation with God, and I truly didn't want to see a brother in Christ "go out like that!" Meaning, I saw his "state of being" as truly degraded and out of communion with God. Yes, he probably went to church somewhere, and he was back at Rev. class, but he had very much fallen out of God's graces. This is clear from all the scriptures I cited. And my prayers with this woman of God and several other prayer warriors were so much focused on his repentance and restored relationship with God, that I actually had a burden for him as my Christian brother. I wanted to see him do right by God, by me, and for the restoration of my hope in him as the person I had originally thought he was. This was my last hope, and it was the biggest. I couldn't have that one come crashing down! That would mean that he really was the con artist that I had begun to think that he was, and that hence, if he fooled me, that means I'm a fool!

So it defines me as a fool in the past and present, but I wasn't going to let it define my future. Those last few months of the year really did make me assess my future and to what extent I wanted a new man in it. With me being 55, I assessed that I'd much rather put my time, emotions and resources into fulfilling other areas of my life than marriage.

Yes, I want a relationship, but not a marriage. I had already put my life on hold for the best years of my life, waiting on a husband for 15 years! Now, I'd really rather invest my heart and emotions into something else like entrepreneurship and travel! I've already concluded that remarriage is no longer a goal, and I'm actually fine with that. For a decade and a half, I was obsessed with wanting to be settled down in a happy marriage. Then I finally get a marriage for a half-second, and I come out wanting no part of it any time soon. I just have to make sure that it isn't out of hurt or bitterness. I do believe that it is out of practicality and just being honest about my stage of life.

Thank God that He sent me a man with whom I don't have to wonder, or have trust issues. He is a man I've known since I was 14! This is the most wonderful man I've ever dated, and I know that he is for real, because I knew him well... well before we became an item! I know him and even my dad knew his dad (who was his business attorney) and family of attorneys and judges. Trustworthiness isn't even an issue; it's already been proven! This man IS who he portrays himself as... the most wonderful man ever! And God has used this man to affirm my worth and to make up for all the hurt and pain and rejection and neglect of the last two marriages... even with such a short time together! God HAS "redeemed the time and restored what the locusts have eaten"! Hallelujah! So I won't worry about marriage and the future; I'm just enjoying and appreciating whom He's given me! Isn't it just GOD, who brought me just the right man, wrapped up in just the right circumstances, to circumvent those seemingly insurmountable circumstances of trust issues! And to think that God brought me this right man all along – even before I got caught up with the wrong man! But I just didn't know better!

*But back to my statement that I had literally put my heart into it; I was so much vested in this "hope against all hope" that God would move on Dick's heart and have him do the right thing, that when Dick refused, I began to experience anxiety, ultimately sending my blood pressure to stroke level. I remember the day that he canceled our meeting, how devastated I felt, even physically. Then for the next few days, I actually felt my blood pressure rising. I got my monitor out and started checking it daily. It was high and continuing to creep up. And I remember vividly my acute anxiety the day in late December when Dr. Z. texted me about Dick's change of meeting plans. This anxiety sent my blood pressure up even more. Further exacerbating my anxiety was the fact that I knew I'd have to get a doctor appointment very quickly, since I had learned that Dick had cut me from his health insurance (even though he was supposed to have left me on until the divorce); so I got an* appointment for 12/31. But in the meantime it continued to go up very high until I had a TIA the morning of my appointment, then a stroke the next day, followed by another TIA!

I literally took these matters to heart! I wish that I knew how to care less (you know that phrase: "I could care less!"?). I am a very empathetic person, and I wear my heart on my sleeve. This is a precarious place for a heart – it is out there exposed to get hurt real easily. So Dick's betrayal during and after our marriage didn't just hurt – it devastated!

I was too available; even after the marriage was over, I was emotionally available. A "normal" wife would have put her foot down and would not have stood for some of his stuff. Like that wedding night when I found out that he was impotent! Yeah, I should have been out of there! What normal person would put up with that? Again, I was a too vested! A fool in love! Even months into the sexless, sleepless marriage, instead of lying in bed being made love to, I'd lie there awake due to his snoring, just loving him and accepting the lack of a love life! Again, I was a fool! This is more than wearing my heart on my sleeve; this is just being a fool! I didn't know the difference, but I do now.

We Christians keep wrongly assuming that turning the other cheek means taking the neglect or abuse and letting God deal with our pain. And since patience is a fruit of the Spirit, we think we're to endure a wrong situation that we never should have been in. We try to find God in it. God was never in this union because it was based on a lie from the beginning. Dick could never even consummate a marriage and never intended to be a financial contributor. This is not a husband; this is a fraudster! God did not send him!

But I hadn't yet defined it as the wrong situation at the time of the marriage, because I was still so hopeful and optimistic. It's good to be these things, but not when you're applying them to the wrong set of circumstances! I had the wrong man, but didn't recognize it! So <u>I never should have been optimistic for the right results with the wrong man!</u> Now if he were physically abusing me, then I'd know he was the wrong one immediately! I would have been so out of there! But, since he presented himself as such a sweet guy and kept giving me excuses, I didn't see the emotional abuse and that he was a user and not into me. Once I gained the right perspective, I took the proper measures!

Perspective is so important. I coined this expression many years ago: <u>"What you believe can constrain you; what you believe can set you free! Choose your beliefs wisely!"</u> My unwise beliefs led me to stay in that marriage ten months too long! Now, with the right perspective, I feel so free, so grown, so clean and clear thinking!

*So, back to that Sunday morning in bed: My two take-aways were that my wounds were down to my soul and that I was still holding out hope for him making amends. Yes, even after he canceled our meetings last year. And even after I had a stroke four months ago as result of my emotional anguish over betrayal, I still held out. But I realize that this was due to something that happened a few months ago.*

*In February, after Dr. Z. and some class members had come to visit me after my stroke, Dr. Z. had told Dick of their visit, and so he called me and asked to visit. I told him that we could visit, but not here at the house, because it would just feel too uncomfortable. I told him that we can meet elsewhere and that I'd like to have someone present. He agreed and said he'd make the arrangements and get back with me. Well folks, I hate to admit it, but I believed him again* and held out hope for three months after that! It was another chance for him to redeem himself and for my hope in men to be restored. But again, he never, ever meant for it to happen.

More specifically, my realization of my still holding out hope came as a result of remembering the last conversation I had with Dr. Z. He had called me in March to ask me to teach at his women's conference in October. I responded that I could not commit to that, because I wasn't even resuming my Rev. classes with him due to Dick's return. I told him that I was awaiting our meetup that Dick had agreed to, so that we could first make amends before I felt comfortable returning to a class that Dick attended. He said he'd talk to Dick about having that meeting. In April, Dr. Z. called again with the same request, and I reiterated the same.

Dr. Z. made an ordeal out of my not wanting to meet with Dick at my house. I felt that this was ludicrous; I explained that if it is uncomfortable to have a certain person in my house, then I don't have to have them over! This is my right! I tried to get Dr. Z. to see that the real problem was not where to meet; Dick just didn't want a third party present. He knew that a third party would insist on accountability. But Dr. Z. didn't see this; he was just critical of the fact that I wouldn't have Dick over! He said I perhaps hurt Dick's feelings by saying this! This was very revealing of his bias, because Dr. Z., who is a certified therapist as well as teacher, was willing to give Dick yet another excuse – once again enabling Dick! And Dr. Z. knows that Dick owes me a great deal of money, so he was in effect putting Dick's "feelings" ahead of his "responsibility" for debt repayment. The Bible doesn't command us to "Owe no man...," except for if your feelings are hurt!

Then Dr. Z. ended the conversation saying that Dick won't meet with me unless I let him come to my house! Again, I don't understand why he believes it's Dick's prerogative and why he is willing to do Dick's bidding! Well, I do know that Dick's ploy of innocence and charm ingratiates him wherever he goes! So perhaps it even worked on Dr. Z. Well this is my home, and I have reasons for not inviting him here! The superficial reasons are that I didn't want to have to try to fix myself and the house up to receive company. Since I had been recovering at home, I wasn't on top of housework or my appearance. And generally speaking, if the parting was unpleasant, you certainly don't want to receive your ex in your house, potentially bringing that unpleasantness (or at least the unpleasant memories) with him. Especially if you're a sensitive person such as I, who wears her heart on her sleeve. I had already symbolically purged my home of the emotional garbage in this house from his past presence. There are memories of the unfortunate encounters I had with him in each of the rooms, so I had to work hard to overcome them after all these months. So to have him march back up in here would, in an emotional sense, undo all the progress that I had made.

And since the premise of the visit would be my well-being, then he'd have to fully address my well-being, which would bring the conversation around to his betrayal and the debt issue. Well think about it; this is where we had all our arguments about money. He wouldn't talk about it then, so what makes me believe he'll talk about it now without resorting to his "head wagging", his raising his voice and his denial of financial responsibility (which is why I had requested a third party)! And why would I want to bring this negativity back up in this place? I wouldn't, and I won't! And remember, I am still recovering from a stroke, which was induced by the stress and anxiety of this man and his betrayal. I am not going to do something that would bring on any more stress. Then, there's the pretense. He would want to come up in here acting like he is concerned about my health; after all, that was the pretense of his "visit"! If he were concerned about me, he would have been the husband that God calls men to be. But in light of his failure to do so, his "visit" should include making financial amends. This is the same reason that I won't return to class with him. I don't do pretense; so either we talk and mend ways, or we don't sit in each other's presence acting as though things are fine between us. So, (in my mind I'm saying to Dr. Z.) this is why I'm not going to have this man in my house or go to class with him.

Well, Dick is game playing. He knows that I'm not going to agree to have him over; so he can now tell Dr. Z. that he tried, but I won't meet with him. Well, he can fool man, but he can't fool God. And God will deal with a fool! Dick has it coming to him! But I can't let my health suffer as a result of Dick's hard heart. I had prayed for his hard heart, but prayer is not manipulation of God's hand. All God will do is knock; that person has to open the door!

So, back to that conversation with Dr. Z. that led me to understand that I was still holding out hope: I had told Dr. Z. that I did not receive his profession that Dick would only meet with me at my house. This was because I trusted that God would make a way since God would want Dick to make amends. Yet, a couple of weeks later, I lay in bed that Sunday morning being reminded of it by the Holy Spirit. This was a morning where God wanted to reveal to me an important truth that would peel off yet another layer on that onion. He revealed to me that my very statement of refusal to receive Dr. Z.'s profession was evidence that I still had not let go of an unreal expectation, and hence my state of blues, tears, and blood pressure spikes. That morning, before even rising, my pressure was high, and it stayed that way until after church. I remember still going through the "letting go" process while in church and weeping throughout prayer time. I know that it is a cliché, but I had to "Let go and let God!"

## Chapter 24: "I FINALLY GOT IT!"

*June 23rd, 2015*

This is exactly one year from the letter dated June 23, 2014, that I printed out and took to my therapist's office last year to read to my husband and my therapist. [It gave my insights leading up to my conclusion that we must separate.] And what a journey I've gone on since then! I must say that I was naïve to think that it would be smooth sailing... that cutting out the tumor that had grown in my life would be the end of it. But it was only the beginning!

I'm kind of in the mood to summarize my reflections, revelations and resolutions on this journey using this metaphor. The way I would characterize it is that, this tumor had metathesized; thus, his ways had worked their way into other areas of my life. One of the areas that it spread to was my finances. When he stopped paying his debt to me, it made me unable to pay these bills. These were large expenses that I never would have charged to my card alone. My habit had been to purchase only what I could pay off monthly. I'd never carried a balance before. Up until he left, he had slowly been paying down the credit card debt that he had agreed to pay, but little did I know that he really lacked the honor and integrity to carry on with those payments. I really had expected more of him. And really, I had thought that we would go on being friends. I thought that by getting rid of the obstacle of the marriage (that could never really be a marriage), we could actually go back to the friendship we'd enjoyed just ten months before. I was actually looking forward to a renewed relationship with him... just not a romantic one. So, to go on the next few months without my friend and without my money was a rude awakening. Compounding it was the fact that it was my "friend" who stiffed me for a great deal of money! So I had to question whether he ever was a "friend". Was I being played? Had I been played all along? But I wouldn't let "yes" be the answer to those questions. I kept giving excuses for my "friend". When friends told me that he'd never pay me back, I actually refuted them for an entire year! I was a fool for an entire year!

Now, granted though, late last year I did finally come to the realization that he had played me. I realized that he was completely devoid of the honor and integrity that I thought he had and that he would not voluntarily repay me (so I prayed for his conviction to repay me). In fact, the realization of his betrayal was directly attributable to the anxiety and stress that led to my TIAs and stroke the very last day of last year. I remember when it finally sank in and how I felt in my body when I finally realized what it truly was... "betrayal!" That's a hard pill to swallow. I could say that I was "defrauded" all day long, but I wouldn't let myself admit that I was "betrayed". Once I finally admitted that to myself, I can remember that my anxiety swelled, and I could feel my blood pressure rising for the two weeks leading up to my TIAs and stroke. So this is the other area to which this "tumor" metathesized... my health! He affected my health and my wealth! But I allowed it.

[It is always useful to discover your complicity in any victimization so that you won't repeat the same mistake; so that you can reach yet another Revision Decision. Here's a lesson I learned about how I had "allowed it":]

Just when I thought that my journaling was through, God opened the door to more insight that I received only this morning when a friend called me. I finally got it! Through our conversation, I finally understood that I had allowed it! I allowed the defeat! She had a very frank conversation with me that was definitely Holy Spirit led. I had actually run into this friend three days ago at the 25$^{th}$ Annual Juneteenth Celebration in Pomona [founded by Trudy Coleman], and we sat and talked for two and a half hours straight! I call her my friend now, but then, she was a lady whom I'd met at our Rev. class and with whom I'd had only one conversation. She truly ministered to me that day and today, and I told her this morning that I am taking her forward in my life as my friend and that we will stay in each other's lives!

That day, my new friend Deborah had shared with me that she too had overcome a stroke. She talked about how the stress of her marriage had also been a contributing factor. She told me that she had been praying for me and that in fact, her prayers had extended back over a year ago, when we had had our first conversation. She stated that she could see back then that I was highly stressed and that I was trying so hard to mask it that I was very "robotacle". Wow! I had no idea that I was coming off like that! How truly perceptive of her; I would most definitely attribute that to the Holy Spirit, because in my conversations with her, I can see that she is a woman who walks with God! She said that she felt that something was going on, and she started praying for me back then. Also, once it was announced in Rev. class that I had had a stroke, she said that she felt that she was supposed to have called me, but didn't follow the Holy Spirit's leading as she should have, but has learned that she should follow through from now on.

Well, she did follow through, because on yesterday, she texted me saying, "I think I may have a few more things to say to help soothe your heart," and she called me this morning and shared them. Thank God for sisters like this! First of all, again, through the Holy Spirit, she perceived that my heart needed soothing. She recognized that I didn't just suffer a physical stroke, but that I had suffered a blow to my heart, and that such a hurt and a heavy heart can lead to physical illness. And she knew that, although I was much better, my heart was still in need of soothing. She also shared that she knew that I was better from seeing my countenance when we saw each other three days ago. She said that I looked so good and refreshed and happy! This was as opposed to the countenance that I had over a year ago when we first spoke. At that time, I was still in the throes of the confusion of the farce of a marriage I had found myself in. And unbeknownst to me, it was showing up on my face and in my behavior.

So, what Deborah shared with me this morning was that "God will not allow others to get victory over us," yet while she continued talking, the Holy Spirit filled in the rest, which was that: "If it 'seems' that another has gotten victory over me, then that is because 'I' have allowed it!" Whoa!

What? But I understood it in an instant. I told her that today marks exactly a year when Dick and I sat in front of the counselor, and I shared that we must separate. And I continued to share that though the next few months afterwards I was fine, by the end of the year I had found myself hurt by his betrayal of withholding my repayment and our continued friendship. It "seemed" that he had gotten victory over me, and I was bewildered and even hurt more by this. Not to mention the blow I had gotten in November in court, when the commissioner wouldn't hear my statements and twisted it to make me the one out to get money! I continued to "feel" defeated from then, through December which is when I had finally called the betrayal what it was; even more so after I had the TIAs and stroke! I have felt defeated for too long! I had to go back and correct the prior sentence; I had typed, "I have 'been' defeated...," but that is the very issue that I'm writing about! I "have not been and am not" defeated! I just "feel" defeated! Big difference, and that's what I'm journaling about today.

### I AM NOT DEFEATED!

I let my feeling of defeat equal defeat! I let myself believe that because I felt defeated, I was defeated! This is a lie from the pit of hell! I AM NOT DEFEATED! If the Bible says "The righteous will not be forsaken," then I won't. That means, that even if I feel like I've been forsaken, I'm not... it just appears that way! So Dick has nothing over me! It may seem that he has gotten away with not repaying me over $11k dollars [almost half of which was credit card debt; over half was pre-marital funds], and yes, that's a big sum to be out of, but look... God HAS provided! And yes, I've amassed hundreds of dollars of interest payments, having to leave such a large sum of debt on the credit card, but I've still managed bills, eaten, laughed, played, danced, prayed and ministered – as God would have it! I have a sound mind and the use of my limbs, which seems to be a platitude that we hear from Christians when testifying, but I truly have this as my testimony... post stroke! I was not left with a limp or a slur, but with pep in my step... literal too, because I Chicago step better than before! And my mind is sharp and perceptive to the Holy Spirit. We know that the Holy Spirit's imparted knowledge is far superior to anybody's IQ anyway! Hallelujah!!!!

I've been telling myself lately that "I am too blessed to be stressed!" I repeat it, not as a cute saying, but as the truth about my life! I have soooooo much for which to give God the glory! And on top of His blessings to my health and wealth (in spite of...), He has also given me material blessings! I have a retirement fund which pays my mortgage, a nice home, a big enjoyable yard with a pool, a fine car, and all the amenities I need. And of course, I have the priceless blessings of salvation, the Holy Spirit, health, my two wonderful and beautiful grown kids, all my siblings, my friends and a great man in my life.

So, not only am I not defeated, but I am blessed! God has a plan to redeem the time and to give back what the locusts (Dick has) have eaten. And I am the head and not the tail, above and not beneath, the lender and not the borrower! I was just confessing these scriptures this morning, and then Deborah called and stated the same! She stated these scriptures, as well as the essence of them, stating that I will get my money back; maybe not from Dick, but from God through other means! He will get the money back to me many times over! We're all setting ourselves up for God's promises, good or bad. Either we are righteous and have suffered loss, but will get back what the locusts ate; or we are like Dick, who is only setting himself up for God's promise of vengeance for wronging a brother or sister. God's got this! So shame on me for fretting, worrying, stroking out over it, and feeling defeated! I have the victory! And the person who wronged me has the promise of the wrath of God!

So, back to my statement that "If someone has seemed to get victory over me, it is because I have allowed it": I didn't allow the incident, but I allowed how I processed the incident! I labeled it as looking like defeat, feeling like defeat, and stressing out and being anxious as though in defeat (which did defeat my cardiovascular system; but only temporarily and mildly, thank God!). But then I continued in defeat for half a year longer! We are responsible for our actions <u>as well as our reactions</u>! My reaction to someone else's action was to be anxious and to stress out. Philippians 4:6, 7 says, "Do not be anxious about anything, but in every situation, by prayer and petition, with thanksgiving, present your requests to God. And the peace of God, which transcends all understanding, will guard your hearts and your minds in Christ Jesus." I did the prayer part, and I did the petition part, but unfortunately, I did the "anxious" part. Therefore, my mind wasn't guarded, so I took on defeat;

and my heart wasn't guarded, so I took on a heavy heart, leading to a stroke!

Well God knows Dick far better than I do, and He knew that all the prayers of all the sisters in Christ I had agreeing with me would not change his hard heart. God knew Dick would even fake it and agree to meet, but really was never planning to follow through. So God's resolution is going to have to be something different. He will get money into my hands by different means and will deal with His hard-hearted son.

But meanwhile, I stressed out, stroked out, and missed out! I responded with foolish beliefs, not faithful beliefs. So, back to my original statement, "What a fool I was!" Due to today's conversation with Deborah, I have a lot of insight into how this happened. The Holy Spirit kept downloading thoughts and conclusions into me hours after our conversation, and one key conclusion is that my naivety stems back to my childhood. But I always thought it was optimism, which is good, right? Well, it can kind of get out there to the point where it is unrealistic and naïve. And then couple that with my strong sense of fairness and justice... it can lead to very unrealistic expectations.

But you see, I never had this sense of fairness and justice shaken until adulthood. I never had anything to rock my world; to turn it upside down; to tarnish my faith in God or make me question Him, or to relinquish my sense of fairness and justice until adulthood. I never had a loss, my parents never split up, I've never been poor, never had trauma, sickness, bullying, poor self-esteem, abuse, never saw abuse, etc. Everything in my childhood, teen years and young adult years was exceptional. I had a great family, upbringing and opportunities.

Because of this, I also learned to give everyone the benefit of the doubt and not even recognize ill-intent for what it is. I would say that my parents sheltered my sister and me, and the Lord shielded and guarded me from pain and problems all those years. I thank God for this, and yet I thought that's how life was... everything works out if you're in the right. Justice is served, everything is reconciled, all wrongs are rectified, and all is fair. You don't play in the dirt... none gets on you... so I thought. But that's not true in life. <u>Sometimes dirt is blown on you, and sometimes dirt is thrown on you!</u> Bad things do happen to good people.

There are people who grow up with bad things happening to them and all around them all the time, thus they've learned coping skills and how not to let their expectations get the best of them. Some people, to their detriment, learn not to have any expectations at all, which is the other end of the spectrum. Balance is key to so many things in life, and the lack of it can be problematic. At my overly optimistic extreme end of the spectrum, I was unable to even process the things that hit me in adulthood, much less respond adequately and in a timely fashion. Case in point: My response to the sexless marriage to Dick was inadequate and too slow. I should have processed that he had committed fraud from the beginning and thus annulled the marriage immediately.

So, reflecting back on my childish thinking that bad things don't happen to good people, I realized that even in the present, I consider this to be God's M.O. Yes, I took that thinking into adulthood as to what I should trust God to do. <u>In other words, my faith wasn't in God to do what He does, but in Him to do what I projected on Him to do – earthly justice!</u> So my prayers had no wiggle room for God not bringing justice, because if He is a just God, then justice will be served – case closed.

This explains why I always had a problem with people inserting in prayers, "If it is Your will, Lord." Didn't we just pray for justice, which <u>is</u> His will? Then why question His will? Well, what I have just learned is that though justice is His will, heavenly justice and earthly justice may look like two totally different things. So what I thought was faith wasn't faith at all. Let me put it in mathematical terms, since I love math. I used the associative theory of faith. If God equals justice, and rectifying wrongs equals justice, then God is a rectifier of wrongs. Well, even if this is true, how He rectifies them can be so different from the way we pray that it would happen. Therefore, we really should pray, "Thy will be done," and "If it is Your will, Lord." So my faith should be in God reconciling things in His own heavenly way, with His heavenly account and His "cattle on a thousand hills"! <u>My faith should be in His hand to move, not on my desired outcome.</u>

So, in the instance of my prayers for God to rectify Dick's wrongs, what I thought was faith turned out to be faith infused with my sense of human justice. As I stated earlier, I equated what I had perceived to be the right outcome based on earthly fairness with God's heavenly righteousness. Therefore, I earnestly was surprised at my treatment in the courtroom. I was in the right. Dick was in the wrong. God knows it, so He'll have justice served in the courtroom. How naïve. Likewise, when my sisters and I prayed for softening of Dick's heart to do the right thing, I had faith that it would happen because God is able and willing. So even when I didn't have favor in court in November, I totally expected to have favor through prayer in December. But since God gives us volitional minds, if Dick wanted to continue being a dick about it and blow off our meeting, then God would just take care of it in His own way.

When I was on the phone with Deborah this morning, another thing stood out to me. She flat out said, "He will never pay you back your money!" Yet I didn't start reproving her, saying, "I don't receive that!" like I did with my other friends who'd made the statement over the past year. Again, I had made these statements for a year in "faith" that God would move on Dick. If I don't believe this, then I don't have faith, right? Wrong. I should have faith that "God's got me!" However He so choses, God will take care of me and has done so already. She went on to say just that. So this marked real spiritual growth for me, and I told her this. I finally got it. A year ago I had asked Dick for the money back, but I will not expect a penny back willingly. But God knows every penny that Dick owes me and will hold him accountable to the very end... and beyond, because he will spend eternity in the presence of God who knows all. He is only bankrupting his own heavenly account, as Deborah put it.

So, I've come full circle in this year since my letter of exactly one year ago. I went back and viewed that nine-page document and reflected on how hurt yet optimistic I was. I've copied below the closing lines of that letter that show that I was reaching out in hope of something that wasn't coming... restitution. Yet a year later, I have still been expecting it.

*"...he should have come to me and said, 'Now it's time for me to repay you, because you paid for my obligations when we were dating, and it put you out of THOUSANDS of dollars. Here's a start dear, and there's more to come each month!' This is not just a fantasy – if he is a real husband, he would do this! Even someone who is not a spouse, who made a person forfeit their money, should make amends!*

*This is just a deep wound that has been wide open for nine months, and only Dick can close it. I need Dick to close this wound in me...!"*

I wouldn't have thought it would have taken me a year to grow, but at least I have. On today, June 23, 2015, I profess that I reject the previous expectations. I don't expect him to willingly repay me, and I don't expect him to heal my wounds! God is my healer! Thank you God for healing me, even today! I embrace the blessings that you have for me, God. Thank you Jesus, I'm walking into my blessings!

*Sunday, January 31st, 2016*

*It has been half a year since I've journaled, and longer than that since I've worked on my book! I looked back at my June 2015 entry, and I realized that I'm done with this journaling process! I had finally peeled back that last layer of that stinky onion, and I'm done with the healing process! I thank you God!!!!!!! You've brought me through a long journey, but I'm on the other side now! No, not concerning the recovery of my funds. The divorce and judgment were granted on October 29, 2015 (for only half of the marital debt), but Dick hasn't paid me a dime to this day. But I'm in the process of garnishing his wages. No, my healing wasn't about the money. My emotional healing was linked to my spiritual enlightenment, and Lord, you did that through the many sisters who prayed and talked with me and through the Holy Spirit who poured out revelations and resolutions to me through my journaling process! Thank you, Father, and thank you my sisters!*

As to why I haven't even worked on my book in so long, I recall how I had taken a detour in March when I decided that I'd learn all I could about the root cause of hypertension; so I enrolled in "YouTube University" for a few months! LOL! Then I hosted exchange students for several months, and then I enrolled in a business class for entrepreneurs and started my own consulting business! [Fletcher Enterprises provides outsourced services such as project management, needs assessment, feasibility studies, quality assurance, compliance management, grant writing and editing.] I never got back on course with my book until... today; but at least I was ultra-productive last year in other areas, thank God! And my relationship with Stan is still great, and we did a lot of fun things together in 2015, including his birthday gift of taking me to see Janet Jackson!

Today, in church, Sister Tatum asked me how my book was coming along. She and Sister Claudette have been my cheerleaders. I thank God for that confirmation... I need to get back to this. Pastor Ken also confirmed (late last year) that I was to get back to it. When he as anointing those who came forward, he spoke a "Word of Knowledge" over me... that my book won't do anyone any good unless it's finished! So, let's get back to work!

I just looked at my last work on the construction of the book, and frankly, it looks daunting. But it isn't. If it appears difficult and I avoid it, then I'm doing something wrong. Holy Spirit, this is your project... your idea; please show me how to complete it joyfully! And please don't let the emotional subject matter bring me down. Amen.

*March 1st, 2016*

Isn't it something that today, as I was going over my journal in the editing process, I read the notes for March 1st, 2014, and it stated that today is the day that we finish playing HHX catch up (but there was still plenty CC debt before and after that point)! Wow; if only! And on this March 1st, two years later, I am still chasing down that debt! [Wage garnishment for half the debt hasn't gone through yet.] Worse than an infidel!

*Thursday, March 31st, 2016*

Wow! This morning I just finished editing my book! I'm finished! It took me exactly two months from two entries above. Well I feel very good about the outcome! It is good material, and I truly believe that it will be a blessing to many women and men who are going through, and many more who can take heed from my revelations and not have to go through. I believe that my revelations from the Holy Spirit are universal enough to help anyone in fact, whether in a relationship or not. Lord, I pray that you bless this book – fiercely – to do just that. And I thank you for taking my mess of a marriage and making it a message to many! God Bless!

Sunday, May 1st, 2016

How ironic! It was exactly two years ago that I began this journaling process, and it is today that I am ending it! It was cathartic, it was the catalyst for change, and therefore it was a blessing. Through it, I received emotional healing and spiritual closeness to the Lord.

Ironically, this is also the day that the first wage garnishment for debt repayment should take effect. Hallelujah! Though it's only for a portion of the marital debt, the pre-marital debt remains... but God's got me!

Lastly, this is the month that I publish this book! Though I went through a mess of a marriage, I am grateful to be able to share my message with you! May God richly bless you in every way!

[I had a feeling that I hadn't written my last journal entry! About a week into May, I checked on the status of my wage garnishment; I found out that my garnishment has to stand in line! Yes! Dick owes others who executed their wage garnishment prior to mine! This man has defrauded others before me, which is no surprise! I inquired as to how long I must wait for the execution of my garnishment, and I was told years! This means that whomever Dick owes, it's a great deal of money! Though I am disgusted, I am not surprised! Dick didn't get this good at getting out of paying his bills by just starting with me! He's been at this for a while!

That's okay, though. God is a god of justice! Justice will be served! And my God will supply all my needs according to His riches in glory! Amen!]

www.ingramcontent.com/pod-product-compliance
Lightning Source LLC
Chambersburg PA
CBHW071310110426
42743CB00042B/1245